TRICIA ALLEY

WHEN SPIRITS CLASH

UNCOVERING THE ALIEN REPTILE

When Spirits Clash: Uncovering the Alien Reptile
By Tricia Alley © Copyright 2022
All rights reserved.

Unless otherwise noted, all Scripture quotations marked are from the Holy Bible, New Living Translation copyright © 1996, 2004, 2007 by Tyndale House Foundation. Used by permission of Tyndale House Publishers Inc., Carol Stream, IL 60188. All rights reserved. New Living, NLT, and the New Living Translation logo are registered trademarks of Tyndale House Publishers.

Scripture quotations marked (NASB) are taken from the NEW AMERICAN STANDARD BIBLE®, Copyright © 1960, 1962, 1963, 1968, 1971, 1972, 1973, 1975, 1977, 1995 by The Lockman Foundation. Used by permission.

Scripture quotations marked (NKJV) are taken from the New King James Version®. Copyright © 1982 by Thomas Nelson, Inc. Used by permission. All rights reserved.

Published by Exodus Christian Book Publishing
www.ExodusChristianBookPublishing.com

Cover and Interior Design by Exodus Design Studio
www.ExodusDesign.com

ISBN: 9780578358390

Printed in the United States of America

DEDICATION

To my friends and family
who've given words of encouragement,
and to those, who with the innocence of children, still ask,
"Who, why, what, when and where?"

TABLE OF CONTENTS

CHAPTER ONE
What on Earth is a Reptilian?

I have to confess that I'm not a science-fiction fan. I could probably count on one hand the number of sci-fi movies I've watched in an entire year! My lack of exposure to the heights of alien imagination, most likely, is the reason I'm fascinated to learn many people do believe alien reptiles live among us. Equally shocking is the belief that these reptiles, called Reptilians, are rich and powerful lizard people who constantly devise plans to control everyone!

What do I do? Like any other red-blooded American, I pick up my Smartphone, google *Reptilian* and consult Wikipedia for the answer of all answers! This is what Wikipedia tells me:

> **Reptilians** (also called **reptoids**,[1] **lizard people**,[2] **reptiloids, saurians, Draconians**)[3][4][5] are purported reptilian humanoids that play a prominent role in fantasy, science fiction, ufology, and conspiracy theories.[6][7] The idea of reptilians was popularised[*sic*]

by David Icke, a conspiracy theorist who claims shape-shifting reptilian aliens control Earth by taking on human form and gaining political power to manipulate human societies. Icke has claimed on multiple occasions that many of the world leaders are, or are possessed by, so-called reptilians.[1]

Phew! It sounds like Reptilians don't actually exist. They're just fictional characters—the creation of someone's imagination that's gone viral. Then I saw an article written by The Atlantic titled, "12 Million Americans Believe Lizard People Run Our Country". The article also states that a poll shows 90 million Americans believe aliens exist and 66 million believe aliens landed at Roswell in 1948.[2]

In addition to this article, there are countless writings about these humanity-destroying, shape-shifting, highly intelligent *Reptilians* who are also known as *Lizard People*. Incredibly ridiculous, right?

Hold on, before we dismiss all this as fantasy and file the imaginations of these people away in our subconsciousness under *psychos* or *conspiracy theorists*, I would like to bring up the fact that Christians also believe in an alien reptile who desires to take over the world and harm humanity. Whoa! That thought came out of nowhere and hit me between the eyes with an impact leaving me with a deep desire to dig into biblical history and search for the *ancient reptile* in order to see how he relates to the *Reptilians* that many believe exist today.

WHAT ON EARTH IS A REPTILIAN?

Before jumping in, for those who may not be familiar with the Bible, I'd like to quickly cover some information about its origin. The ancient writings found in the Bible document God's creation, His relationship with humans, and the establishment of the Jewish and Christian faiths. This group of books were written by many authors beginning some 6000 years ago and spans approximately 3000 years up to around 70 A.D. By the way; our years are marked by B.C., which means *Before Christ* and A.D. meaning *Anno Domini* or *in the year of our Lord* which marks the approximate birth of Jesus. So, 3000 B.C. would be counted as 3000 years before Christ's birth, and as I am writing this, we are in the year 2020 A.D. or 2020 years after His birth.

The authors of the Bible made hundreds of detailed prophesies, of which approximately 90% have accurately come to pass. It's said there are 1239 prophesies in the Old Testament and 578 in the New for a combined total of 1817. The only prophecies that remain unfulfilled pertain to the end of humanity and the last days of the earth we know. Throughout centuries, the consistent truths of biblical prophecies have given validity to the authors' writings.

The book of Genesis, the oldest book of the Bible, talks about creation and the beginning of humanity. It was shortly after creation that the villain of the Bible revealed himself to humans. Surprisingly, this villain first appeared in the form of a deceiving, controlling, shape-shifting *Reptile*! Who was the original *Reptilian*? He was none other than Satan, also known as Lucifer! This is fascinating when we consider that millions of people today are convinced there are political world leaders and elitists who are possessed by shape-shifting alien Reptilians. Ironically, these leaders are also said to be members of a Luciferian religion that carries out Satanic rituals. Does this mean nothing of today has actually changed from 6000 years ago?

In this book, I plan to search the ancient writings of the Bible with the purpose of finding and uncovering Satan as the *Original Reptilian*. I'm filled with many questions such as; "If an alien reptile was real 6000 years ago, are alien Reptilians real today? If so, are they the same beings? Do they have the same goals and purposes? Just what are their goals as they relate to humanity? Where did they come from?" The questions just keep coming!

If you are filled with questions, I hope you will stick around and take this journey with me as I search to uncover the ancient Reptile of the Bible. Now, armed with all my questions, I'm picking up the Bible and turning to the beginning.

CHAPTER TWO
How Did It All Begin?

The Book of Genesis begins with the creation of the sun, moon, earth, man, and all the living creatures. Chapter 1, verse 31 gives insight into the thoughts of God. Unless otherwise specified, all biblical quotes are taken from the NLT (New Living Translation) version.

> [31]*Then God looked over all he had made, and he saw that it was very good! And evening passed and morning came, marking the sixth day.* — Genesis 1:31

God was pleased with His work and considered everything He created to be good. It perfectly aligned with Him. The creation of the first man and woman, Adam and Eve, can be found in Chapter 2 of Genesis, as well as some thought-provoking details about their utopian home called the Garden of Eden. The trees of the garden provided their food, and the man and woman existed in harmony with all animals which were created for their enjoyment. God gave Adam and Eve dominion over all living creatures, and they were meant to live in their perfect environment forever.

Enjoyment of the utopian life came with an exception. God placed a tree in the garden called the "tree of knowledge," of which the two were not allowed to eat. Eating the fruit of this tree would open their eyes to evil, and the presence of evil would cause them to die. God's command to Adam about the "tree of knowledge" is found in verses 16 and 17.

> But the LORD God warned him, "You may freely eat the fruit of every tree in the garden — [17] except the tree of the knowledge of good and evil. If you eat its fruit, you are sure to die." — Genesis 2:16-17

Previously, we read that God considered His creation to be good, and Adam and Eve experienced all the good things created for them in their utopian garden. Therefore, it's reasonable to believe God's command to abstain from the "tree of knowledge" was because He didn't want them to experience evil. This would mean God had full knowledge of the effects of evil prior to creation, and He desired to protect Adam and Eve's innocence.

Interestingly, we can see that God created them with the capacity to choose whether or not to believe He was telling them the truth. Why would He give Adam and Eve the ability to choose if the wrong choice would cause their death? Of course, I can't speak for God, but personally, I can relate to the significance of allowing my loved ones the freedom of choice. I understand love and trust must be freely reciprocated for there to be a meaningful relationship. Anything taken by force is worthless and empty. As a matter of fact, the shear action of force extinguishes trust. It's fascinating to think God created humans with the freedom of choice because He desired to have the same loving and trusting relationships we desire. Many times, throughout the Bible, people were referred to as God's children. This reveals the relationship He wanted was that of a loving parent to innocent children. However, innocence was abruptly extinguished upon the introduction of evil.

It seems every story has a villain. The Bible's villain, in the form of a serpent, entered the scene in chapter three. Using the strategy of divide and conquer, the serpent found Eve alone in the garden and began to ask questions concerning the forbidden fruit. After she answered his questions, he convinced her that if she ate the fruit, not only would she not die, but she would gain understanding and be like God. Who wouldn't want to be like the loving Father she knew, right?

> *The serpent was the shrewdest of all the wild animals the LORD God had made. One day he asked the woman, "Did God really say you must not eat the fruit from any of the trees in the garden?"*
>
> *² "Of course we may eat fruit from the trees in the garden," the woman replied. ³ "It's only the fruit from the tree in the middle of the garden that we are not allowed to eat. God said, 'You must not eat it or even touch it; if you do, you will die.'"*

> ⁴ *"You won't die!" the serpent replied to the woman.* ⁵ *"God knows that your eyes will be opened as soon as you eat it, and you will be like God, knowing both good and evil."*
> — Genesis 3:1-5

Eve believed the serpent and ate the fruit. She then gave it to Adam, who also ate. Immediately, their eyes were opened. Their once pure thoughts became tarnished with the negative emotions of guilt and shame. Adam and Eve had been warned that eating the fruit would cause them to die, but it wasn't instantaneous. Instead, the painful aging process of their bodies began, and death was imminent. Access to the sustaining fruit from the *Tree of Life* was denied, and it became necessary for them to work in order to survive. Adam and Eve's loving and trusting relationship with God was never the same. The rest of their story can be found in Genesis, but in the interest of finding answers to our original questions, let's return to the reptile.

Did you notice the serpent spoke to Eve? If we continue to read, we find the deceptive serpent didn't slither around on the ground while in the Garden of Eden. He walked on legs before he deceived Eve. It was his treachery that caused him to crawl on his belly and live a lowly existence.

> ¹⁴*Then the Lord God said to the serpent, "Because you have done this, you are cursed more than all animals, domestic and wild. You will crawl on your belly, groveling in the dust as long as you live.* — Genesis 3:14

Who was this serpent that purposely wanted to harm Adam and Eve? Turning to the Book of Revelation, which was written approximately 2000 years ago by John, one of Jesus' twelve disciples, we find Satan was the deceiving serpent.

> *⁹This great dragon—the ancient serpent called the devil, or Satan, the one deceiving the whole world—was thrown down to the earth with all his angels.* — Revelation 12:9

Look at that! Satan has angels! The ancient deceiving serpent was also called a dragon and his original dwelling was not on the earth. He sounds like an alien Reptilian kind of guy to me! This captivates the imagination and brings up many questions! Who, or what was Satan, and where did he come from?

We can find answers, but it helps first to understand a concept about Biblical writings. Several Old Testament books and the book of Revelation were written by prophets appointed and anointed by God. God spoke to His prophets, who relayed His messages to the people. When the prophets spoke with authority under God's anointing, it was as though God Himself were speaking through them. Many times, the messages conveyed by the prophets concerned events they would never understand, nor see come to pass during their lifetimes. However, their words were documented to enlighten future generations who have since experienced their prophetic fulfillment.

With this understanding, the prophet Isaiah lived around 700 B.C., which was approximately 2700 years ago. In the Book of Isaiah, the prophet spoke a prophecy concerning the king of Babylon, who was the evil world ruler during the time. While Isaiah was speaking of the king, there was a point where he began to speak directly to Satan, as though he was the force controlling the king. Setting aside the physical human beings, Isaiah and the king of Babylon, the reality was that God was speaking directly to Satan. This means Satan had the ability to manipulate and control the king. In chapter 14, we can see where God began to directly address Satan, who was also known as Lucifer.

> *12 How you are fallen from heaven,*
> *O shining star, son of the morning!*
> *You have been thrown down to the earth,*
> *you who destroyed the nations of the world.*
> *13 For you said to yourself,*
> *'I will ascend to heaven and set my throne above*
> *God's stars.*
> *I will preside on the mountain of the gods*
> *far away in the north.*
> *14 I will climb to the highest heavens*
> *and be like the Most High.'* — Isaiah 14:12-14

There's so much information packed into these verses. The son of light, Lucifer, also called the "star, son of the morning," had his heart set on being king above all of God's stars. Stars refer to angels. If Lucifer was the star of the morning, it would mean he, too, was an angel. Also, we see that God's referred to as the "Most High" or the highest of all beings. Lucifer, a renegade angel, wanted to be like the "Most High" and reign over all the angels, but instead, he has "fallen from heaven" and "been thrown down to the earth."

These verses reveal that God also gave angels the ability to make choices. Lucifer's attempt to take on the Most High failed miserably and resulted in his fall from heaven. It appears the ability to think and choose were essential characteristics that God implanted into all His created beings. Does this mean both the king of Babylon and the serpent from the Garden of Eden chose to allow Satan to control them? That's a fascinating thought. The serpent would have either been a shape-shifted angel or a reptile manipulated by an angel. Genesis 3:1 did say the serpent was the "shrewdest of all the wild animals," which indicates he was capable of devising his own plans. This may explain why God severely cursed that particular reptile as a species.

The previous verses, Isaiah 14:12-14, also gave insight into the relationship God once had with Lucifer. God seemed to experience the emotion of loss over His heavenly angel as He reminded him of all he had given up. God then charged him with having been responsible for destroying all the nations. The question arises as to how and why Satan weakened the nations, but for now, let's look deeper into his attempted takeover of God's kingdom.

CHAPTER THREE
How Did Satan Attempt to Overthrow God's Kingdom?

Typically, what is the first thing a person does when attempting to unseat a leader? He gathers followers, and that's exactly what Satan did. It would seem Satan needed followers from God's creation because he was incapable of creating them for himself. In order to acquire the subjects he so desperately desired, Satan persuaded other angels to join in his rebellion.

Returning to the book of Revelation, we find that Satan was successful in gathering angels to follow him, and these angels were also cast out of heaven. Revelation 12 reveals how all of this went down.

> *⁷Then there was war in heaven. Michael and his angels fought against the dragon and his angels. ⁸And the dragon lost the battle, and he and his angels were forced out of heaven. ⁹This great dragon—the ancient serpent called the devil, or Satan, the one deceiving the whole world—was*

thrown down to the earth with all his angels. —
Revelation 12:7-9

Wow! A war of angels in heaven, and it didn't turn out very well for Satan! Notice he was referred to as a dragon, serpent, devil, and Satan in these short verses. He had many names, but he would never again be called Lucifer, which means God's angel of light. Instead, Satan, the dragon, would be known as the one who goes around deceiving the whole world. Unfortunately, he wasn't alone when cast down to the earth. His renegade army of angels were thrown down along with him.

I have to admit I want to know more about the angel Michael. Mighty Michael, who was powerful enough to throw Satan out of heaven and down to the earth! An interesting thing about the angels is they appeared to have rankings. Obviously, Michael and Satan were powerful angels who had the ability to lead other angels. In the book of Jude, there was a fascinating argument between Michael and Satan that reveals Michael was an archangel, which means *messenger* in Greek. It also appears angels had designated purposes along with their ranks.

> *But Michael the archangel, when he disputed with the devil and argued about the body of Moses, did not dare pronounce against him an abusive judgment, but said, "The Lord rebuke you!"* — Jude 1:9 NASB

Moses was the man God chose to lead the Hebrew

people out of Egypt where the Pharaoh had forced them into slavery for 400 years. If you want to read about their astonishing release and the miracles God performed, the story can be found in the book of Exodus. In this particular exchange, God told Moses to go to the top of a mountain alone because it was time for him to die. He was 120 years old. Satan wanted Moses' body, but God intended for it to go to Michael. Most likely, this was because the people held Moses in such high esteem that the burial of his body would have led them to set up a shrine or monument at his burial site. Historically, shrines and monuments led to the idolization and worship of these inanimate objects. God's plan was for the people to move on from their current location and return to the land He had promised them. Considering Satan was known to be a deceiver, he most likely wanted to use Moses' body in a plot to prevent the people from reaching their intended destination.

Notice Michael didn't rebuke or forbid Satan to have the body of Moses out of his own strength but instead invoked the Lord's name. This means he relied on the power of God, whereas Satan relied on himself. Obviously, Michael, under God's authority, was the stronger of the two.

My next question is, "How big was Satan's army of renegade angels?" In other words, "How many angels were thrown out of heaven and down to earth?"

The only reference to how many angels were cast out of heaven can be found in the Book of Revelation. Revelation is full of symbolism making it difficult to follow. At the time it was written, some 2000 years ago, it revealed past, current, and future events. Within it are most of the unfulfilled biblical prophecies. It's believed the symbolism of Revelation was necessary because it was written a few years after Jesus' crucifixion during a time when Christians were severely persecuted. The prophecies found in the Book of Revelation, if understood, would have been considered a threat to the world ruler's dominion and control over people. The physical and spiritual worlds truly collide in Revelation. While Christians may believe the full word of God as written in the Bible, most shy away from standing against the evil spiritual beings that share our space on earth and in its atmosphere. Mostly, Christians' focus is on the leader, Satan.

With this understanding, we return to chapter 12, where we find verses concerning Satan's fall from heaven and how many angels fell with him.

> ³ Then another sign appeared in heaven: and behold, a great red dragon having seven heads and ten horns, and on his heads were seven crowns. ⁴ And his tail *swept away a third of the stars of heaven and hurled them to the earth. And the dragon stood before the woman who was about to give birth, so that when she gave birth he might devour her Child. — Revelation 12:3-4 NASB

Again, we see the dragon thrown from heaven down to the earth, but when he falls, his tail sweeps a third of the stars with him. The angels were referred to as *stars* in the book of Isaiah. If the dragon swept away a third of the angels with his tail, he most likely had a tremendous following! I can't imagine how many angels were thrown down to the earth. They would also have filled the earth's atmosphere, considering angels can transport themselves!

The nature of the fallen angels would have been that of followers. It stands to reason, since they no longer followed their creator, they would easily fall in line under the command of Satan and continue to carry out his strategies. This intrigues the imagination and brings up an interesting question. With rebellion as a key characteristic of the fallen angels, once they were thrown to the earth, does Satan continue to fight against angelic challenges to his dominion? In view of his character, Satan would definitely recognize the signs of rebellion! It seems reasonable to believe he would use his power and influence to swiftly and brutally extinguish any uprising at the first indication of dissension.

Why would Satan, a powerful angel, bother to control an evil human ruler like the king of Babylon, as we read in Isaiah 14? Pride and vanity were Satan's greatest faults. He convinced himself it was possible for him to be greater than his creator. To be prideful means to lift yourself up. A few characteristics that go along with pride are arrogance, selfishness, self-servitude, greediness, and conceit. Historically, powerful rulers have had no problem with lying, stealing, or murdering to gain riches, conquer nations, and control the masses in order to expand their kingdoms. Does it stand to reason Satan's motives never changed after he was cast to the earth? He wanted to lead the angels, so why wouldn't he want to control humans and grow his earthly kingdom? Genesis 1:6 says God created humans in His own image, and throughout the Bible, we can find His words of love toward humanity. Why wouldn't a defiant, greedy, narcissistic angel want to dominate all of God's creation?

Revelation 12:3-4 raises other questions, such as: Who was the child that Satan desperately wanted to devour? Why did the dragon have seven heads and ten horns? We'll take a look at the identity of the child later; however, studying the symbolism of the dragon and why he had seven heads and ten horns would be too deep for the questions in this book. For the sake of sticking to our subject, we will continue to answer questions concerning Satan and the fallen angels, but first, let's answer a few questions about God.

CHAPTER FOUR
Who is God Besides the Creator?

How does a multi-dimensional God explain Himself to humans who only see the world in three dimensions? The very first verses in Genesis give us an idea.

> ¹*In the beginning God created the heavens and the earth.* ²*The earth was formless and empty, and darkness covered the deep waters. And the Spirit of God was hovering over the surface of the waters.*
> — Genesis 1:1-2

First and foremost, God is a Spirit. What does God, the Spirit, look like? The answer is that we don't know. We can't see Him with our human eyes! Previously, we read Adam and Eve were created in the image of God. We know the body decomposes and ultimately returns to the earth when it dies; however, there has always been a prevalent belief that a part of us never dies. Does this mean the real life, the life that images the creator, is our spirit? This may bring enlightenment as to why we were created with the abilities to think, reason, and choose like the creator. Interestingly, we also have the ability to be creative!

God also described Himself as the Alpha and the Omega, meaning the beginning and the end:

> [8] *"I am the Alpha and the Omega—the beginning and the end," says the Lord God. "I am the one who is, who always was, and who is still to come— the Almighty One." —* Revelation 1:8

We can't fully comprehend when the beginning begins and the ending ends, but we can understand our creation was our beginning and the end, according to the Bible, will be an eternal life for our spirits. It is the spirit that never dies. In addition, the Bible promises our physical bodies will be resurrected from the dead. These new bodies will be eternal and perfect, just as they were when Adam and Eve lived in their utopian Garden of Eden. Later, we'll read more about coming to life again with newly restored bodies, but for now, more about God.

Has God ever presented Himself in human form?
Considering Satan had the ability to transform his image into that of a reptile, it wouldn't be surprising to learn God could manifest Himself into a relatable form to present Himself as human. Even during creation, God the Spirit, had someone with Him working in agreement as they discussed creating Adam.

> [26] *Then God said, "Let us make human beings in our image, to be like us. They will reign over the fish in the sea, the birds in the sky, the livestock, all the wild animals on the earth, and the small*

animals that scurry along the ground." —Genesis 1:26

In the book of John, he wrote about who was with God during creation and called Him the Word and the Light of men.

¹In the beginning the Word already existed.

The Word was with God,

and the Word was God.

² He existed in the beginning with God.

³ God created everything through him,

and nothing was created except through him.

⁴ The Word gave life to everything that was created

and his life brought light to everyone.

⁵ The light shines in the darkness,

and the darkness can never extinguish it. — John 1:1-5

Later, John explained that the Word became a person who was like no other. He was the only begotten of the Father, referring to God.

¹⁴ So the Word became human and made his home among us. He was full of unfailing love and faithfulness. And we have seen his glory, the glory of the Father's one and only Son. — John 1:14

It appears it was this human form who interacted with

Adam and Eve, as can be seen in their first encounter with God after they disobeyed Him.

> *⁸When the cool evening breezes were blowing, the man and his wife heard the LORD God walking about in the garden. So they hid from the LORD God among the trees.* — Genesis 3:8

Adam and Eve heard God walking. In order to make the sound of walking, it seems reasonable that He came to them in a physical form. Could God the Spirit have created a physical form of Himself to serve as a blueprint for humanity for the sole purpose of allowing Him to be physically present with His creation? Does this mean Adam and Eve's decision to believe the serpent separated them from the physical presence of their loving creator? Let's take a look at a couple of instances where the Bible speaks about God appearing in the form of a human.

Abraham was a man who loved God. He followed God's instructions to separate himself and his wife, Sarah, from the evil influences that were prevalent in their homeland. They were to raise a family and establish a people who would choose to know God. Once Abraham had settled in the land God promised him, three men visited him and one of them was the Lord.

> *¹The LORD appeared again to Abraham near the oak grove belonging to Mamre. One day Abraham was sitting at the entrance to his tent during the hottest part of the day. ² He looked up and noticed*

three men standing nearby. When he saw them, he ran to meet them and welcomed them, bowing low to the ground.

³ "My lord," he said, "if it pleases you, stop here for a while. ⁴ Rest in the shade of this tree while water is brought to wash your feet. ⁵ And since you've honored your servant with this visit, let me prepare some food to refresh you before you continue on your journey."

"All right," they said. "Do as you have said."

⁶ So Abraham ran back to the tent and said to Sarah, "Hurry! Get three large measures of your best flour, knead it into dough, and bake some bread." ⁷ Then Abraham ran out to the herd and chose a tender calf and gave it to his servant, who quickly prepared it. ⁸ When the food was ready, Abraham took some yogurt and milk and the roasted meat, and he served it to the men. As they ate, Abraham waited on them in the shade of the trees. — Genesis 18:1-8

The Lord appeared to Abraham in human form. Undoubtedly, He was physically present, so much so, that He ate the food prepared in His honor. Abraham and the Lord conversed while the other two men continued to their intended destination.

¹⁶ Then the men got up from their meal and looked out toward Sodom. As they left, Abraham went with them to send them on their way.

> [17] *"Should I hide my plan from Abraham?"*
> the LORD *asked.* [18] *"For Abraham will certainly be-*
> *come a great and mighty nation, and all the na-*
> *tions of the earth will be blessed through him.* [19] *I*
> *have singled him out so that he will direct his sons*
> *and their families to keep the way of the* LORD *by*
> *doing what is right and just. Then I will do for*
> *Abraham all that I have promised."*
>
> [20] *So the* LORD *told Abraham, "I have heard a great*
> *outcry from Sodom and Gomorrah, because their*
> *sin is so flagrant.* [21] *I am going down to see if their*
> *actions are as wicked as I have heard. If not, I want*
> *to know."* — Genesis 18:16-21

Notice an outcry from Sodom and Gomorrah was heard by the Lord, causing Him to come in physical form to investigate the truth in what was taking place. Normally, people are pretty content as long as they aren't being harmed. Outcry is a strong word indicating that people were suffering or had suffered from evil. We just read why God chose Abraham, and the reason gives insight into God's heart. Verse 19 says God chose Abraham so that he would keep His way. What was God's way? According to these verses, it was to be righteous and just. In this case, God was inundated with people's cries for Him to deal with the injustices inflicted upon them. Most likely, people tolerated and even participated in unsavory practices that eventually crested to an intolerable level of evil. Evil always has victims, and these victims had desperately cried out to

God for justification. It's remarkable that before activating judgment against the guilty, God sought the truth! Does this mean God doesn't really know or keep up with what is going on down on earth? The Bible consistently bears out that God knows the past, present, and future. There's another reason why God wasn't actively involved.

When we apply what we've learned about God, it's feasible to believe He allows people to live their lives and make choices with little interference from Him. However, as in the prior example, there comes a time when He does decide to intervene. The cries of the people compelled Him to take action. Also noteworthy, was the fact He didn't appear to activate judgment against evil lightly. How does a loving Father, who sees the length of human life as a breath of time, bring Himself to judge those He created? Especially when a judgment in favor of one resulted in the harm of another. Only He knows when evil ascends to the point that requires His correction.

The standard for God's judgment rests on the basis of His goodness which existed before creation. It's a standard that goes far beyond humanity's ability to understand or attain. Everyone falls short of the standard of goodness that personifies God. Romans 3:10-18 brings this to light along with some ways humans fail.

> [10] *As the Scriptures say, "No one is righteous—not even one.*
>
> [11] *No one is truly wise; no one is seeking God.*

¹² All have turned away; all have become useless. No one does good, not a single one."

¹³ "Their talk is foul, like the stench from an open grave. Their tongues are filled with lies."

"Snake venom drips from their lips."

¹⁴ "Their mouths are full of cursing and bitterness."

¹⁵ "They rush to commit murder.

¹⁶ Destruction and misery always follow them.

¹⁷ They don't know where to find peace."

¹⁸ "They have no fear of God at all."
— Romans 3:10-18

Sometimes it seems evil people, those deserving of punishment, live a very long time and insatiably cause harm to others. It's astonishing to think God's lack of immediate reaction may be because He is weighing the evilness of the accuser against the evilness of the accused. Though the offenses may differ, they still would be evil by God's standard of goodness.

CHAPTER FIVE
Can All Angels Change
Their Appearance?

There's some fascinating advice found in the book of Hebrews concerning angels.

> ¹ *Keep on loving each other as brothers and sisters.* ² *Don't forget to show hospitality to strangers, for some who have done this have entertained angels without realizing it!*
> — Hebrews 13:1-2

Amazing! We could be kind to a stranger, and that person could actually be an angel! This reveals angels can transform and take on the form of humans. That's wonderful if they're good angels, but pretty disturbing if they want to harm us.

Returning to Genesis chapter 18, where it speaks of the Lord and the two men who came to Abraham in human form, we can learn more about the two men. We know Abraham was amazed as he recognized these men weren't ordinary visitors. When they had finished eating, the Lord stayed to talk to him while the other two men continued on their way to meet with Lot, Abraham's nephew.

> *¹That evening the two angels came to the entrance of the city of Sodom. Lot was sitting there, and when he saw them, he stood up to meet them. Then he welcomed them and bowed with his face to the ground. ² "My lords," he said, "come to my home to wash your feet, and be my guests for the night. You may then get up early in the morning and be on your way again."*
>
> *"Oh no," they replied. "We'll just spend the night out here in the city square."* — Genesis 19:1-2

In these verses, the two men were actually angels. Not only did they have the ability to take on human form, but they also could eat food.

Another occasion when an angelic being appeared in human form, was during the time of the prophet Daniel. Babylon had conquered Judah, the only remaining kingdom of the Israelites. The rest of Israel had long since been overtaken. The Babylonians took the most useful captives as slaves. Those who were allowed to remain in their land, didn't escape the king's control as they were forced to work and pay heavy taxes. Daniel was fourteen when he and three of his close friends, Hananiah, Mishael, and Azariah, were captured. This was the command the king gave concerning the young men:

> [3] *Then the king ordered Ashpenaz, his chief of staff,*
> *to bring to the palace some of the young men of*
> *Judah's royal family and other noble families, who*
> *had been brought to Babylon as captives.* [4] *"Select*
> *only strong, healthy, and good-looking young*
> *men," he said. "Make sure they are well versed in*
> *every branch of learning, are gifted with knowl-*
> *edge and good judgment, and are suited to serve*
> *in the royal palace. Train these young men in the*
> *language and literature of Babylon." [5] The king as-*
> *signed them a daily ration of food and wine from*
> *his own kitchens. They were to be trained for three*
> *years, and then they would enter the royal service.*
> — Daniel 1:3-5

The young men's Hebrew names were changed to those of the Babylonian culture. Daniel became Belteshazzar; Hananiah became Shadrach; Mishael became Meshach, and Azariah became Abednego. The king, who only wanted handsome and healthy servants, commanded they eat his food. Daniel and his friends refused to comply because as Hebrews, they considered some of the food unclean. The king's chief of staff favored Daniel and allowed him to prove he and his friends could eat foods that were acceptable to them without harming their physical appearance. Once satisfied, he allowed them to continue to eat the foods of their choice.

King Nebuchadnezzar was extremely impressed by Daniel's wisdom. He had some very disturbing dreams and demanded his wise men interpret them. In addition to the interpretation, they had to first tell him what he dreamed. God gave Daniel the king's dream and its interpretation through Daniel's own dreams. The king was incredibly grateful, so much so that he rewarded Daniel handsomely with gifts and promotion.

Without a doubt, King Nebuchadnezzar was a vain and prideful man. He had a golden statue built of himself that was ninety feet tall and nine feet wide, and commanded everyone bow down to it when a particular musical instrument sounded. Anyone refusing to comply was burned in a blazing fire. True to their faith to bow only to God, Daniel and his companions ignored the king's command. The wise men, or astrologers, who were envious of the Hebrew men's favor with the king, seized the opportunity and brought charges against Shadrach, Meshach, and Abednego. Daniel wasn't included in the complaint, most likely because he held a higher status than all the wise men. Upon hearing the accusations, King Nebuchadnezzar flew into a rage and ordered the three men brought before him. They stood fast in their refusal to bow to the golden statue, which further incited the king to command they be thrown into the fire. It was while in the fire a fourth man appeared with them. This is how the event transpired.

> [19] Nebuchadnezzar was so furious with Shadrach, Meshach, and Abednego that his face became distorted with rage. He commanded that the furnace be heated seven times hotter than usual. [20] Then he

*ordered some of the strongest men of his army to bind Shadrach, Meshach, and Abednego and throw them into the blazing furnace. *[21] *So they tied them up and threw them into the furnace, fully dressed in their pants, turbans, robes, and other garments. *[22] *And because the king, in his anger, had demanded such a hot fire in the furnace, the flames killed the soldiers as they threw the three men in. *[23] *So Shadrach, Meshach, and Abednego, securely tied, fell into the roaring flames.*

[24] *But suddenly, Nebuchadnezzar jumped up in amazement and exclaimed to his advisers, "Didn't we tie up three men and throw them into the furnace?"*

"Yes, Your Majesty, we certainly did," they replied.

[25] *"Look!" Nebuchadnezzar shouted. "I see four men, unbound, walking around in the fire unharmed! And the fourth looks like a god!"*

[26] *Then Nebuchadnezzar came as close as he could to the door of the flaming furnace and shouted: "Shadrach, Meshach, and Abednego, servants of the Most High God, come out! Come here!"*

*So Shadrach, Meshach, and Abednego stepped out of the fire. *[27] *Then the high officers, officials, governors, and advisers crowded around them and saw that the fire had not touched them. Not a hair* *on their heads was singed, and their clothing was not scorched. They didn't even smell of smoke!*

[28] Then Nebuchadnezzar said, "Praise to the God of Shadrach, Meshach, and Abednego! He sent his angel to rescue his servants who trusted in him. They defied the king's command and were willing to die rather than serve or worship any god except their own God. [29] Therefore, I make this decree: If any people, whatever their race or nation or language, speak a word against the God of Shadrach, Meshach, and Abednego, they will be torn limb from limb, and their houses will be turned into heaps of rubble. There is no other god who can rescue like this!"

[30] Then the king promoted Shadrach, Meshach, and Abednego to even higher positions in the province of Babylon. — Daniel 3:19-30

The king was so astounded by the fourth man's appearance and the miracle that left the three men unscathed, he declared their God was the only one true God. The fourth man could have been an angelic being or the Lord Himself!

Considering the angels have the power to transform their appearance, then it would seem reasonable to believe Satan would also have the same shape-shifting powers. Meaning, the deceiver of the world, who leads a third of the angels, can take on different forms, including that of humans and reptiles, as seen in the book of Genesis.

What are all these angels doing?
A story found in the book of Daniel gives an idea of what angelic beings do in our atmosphere. We just read about Daniel and his three friends' captivity in Babylon. This took place around 600 years before Jesus was born. In chapter 10, we find Daniel was crying out to God because he couldn't understand his distressful dream. He was so disturbed that he fasted and prayed for 21 days as he waited for God to explain it to him. Here is what happened:

> *4 On April 23, as I was standing on the bank of the great Tigris River, 5 I looked up and saw a man dressed in linen clothing, with a belt of pure gold around his waist. 6 His body looked like a precious gem. His face flashed like lightning, and his eyes flamed like torches. His arms and feet shone like polished bronze, and his voice roared like a vast multitude of people.*
>
> *7 Only I, Daniel, saw this vision. The men with me saw nothing, but they were suddenly terrified and ran away to hide. 8 So I was left there all alone to see this amazing vision. My strength left me, my face grew deathly pale, and I felt very weak. 9 Then I heard the man speak, and when I heard the sound of his voice, I fainted and lay there with my face to the ground.*
>
> *10 Just then a hand touched me and lifted me, still*

*trembling, to my hands and knees. ¹¹ And the man
said to me, "Daniel, you are very precious to God,
so listen carefully to what I have to say to you.
Stand up, for I have been sent to you." When he
said this to me, I stood up, still trembling.*

*¹² Then he said, "Don't be afraid, Daniel. Since the
first day you began to pray for understanding and
to humble yourself before your God, your request
has been heard in heaven. I have come in answer
to your prayer. ¹³ But for twenty-one days the
spirit prince of the kingdom of Persia blocked my
way. Then Michael, one of the archangels, came to
help me, and I left him there with the spirit prince
of the kingdom of Persia.* — Daniel 10:4-13

In these verses, Daniel prayed to God, and upon hearing
his prayers, God immediately dispatched an angel to de-
liver an answer. For twenty-one days, another angel, the
prince of Persia, along with his kings, blocked the messenger angel from reaching his destination. Who came to
his rescue? None other than one of God's chief princes, the
mighty warrior angel, Michael.

Opposing angels, with the titles of prince and kings of
Persia, challenged and restrained God's messenger angel.
Persia was the actual world empire during that particular
time in Daniel's life. The angels, although spiritual beings,
had titles pertaining to a real physical territory. This indicates angels have strongholds and can rule over territories
using their angelic power to persuade and control humans.

The prince of Persia obviously held the greater power as he single-handedly restrained God's messenger angel. It was then necessary for multiple angels, or kings of Persia, to hold on to him. It seems angels can resist other angels, restrict their movement, and even force one another to vacate the space they occupy. There was obviously contention between God's heavenly angels and Satan's renegade angels, which caused them to battle in the earth's atmosphere. It seems crucial to Satan and his angels that they prevent the heavenly angel from interacting with Daniel.

Returning to the previous verses, it was the powerful angel, Michael, who sprang into action. Not only did he overcome the prince of Persia, but he also broke off the binding grips of the kings of Persia! It's interesting to imagine the human prince and kings of Persia may have felt their strength leave them for twenty-one days while their evil spiritual controllers were occupied elsewhere!

After the messenger angel had interpreted his dream, Daniel's strength returned, and he composed himself. The angel then conveyed another enlightening message.

> [18] Then the one who looked like a man touched me again, and I felt my strength returning. [19] "Don't be afraid," he said, "for you are very precious to God. Peace! Be encouraged! Be strong!"
>
> As he spoke these words to me, I suddenly felt stronger and said to him, "Please speak to me, my lord, for you have strengthened me."

[20] He replied, "Do you know why I have come? Soon I must return to fight against the spirit prince of the kingdom of Persia, and after that the spirit prince of the kingdom of Greece will come. [21] Meanwhile, I will tell you what is written in the Book of Truth. (No one helps me against these spirit princes except Michael, your spirit prince.

[1] I have been standing beside Michael to support and strengthen him since the first year of the reign of Darius the Mede.) — Daniel 10:18-21 & 11:1

First of all, notice Daniel described the angel's appearance as having a human form. Also, astonishingly, the angel seemed to be in a constant state of battle. His immediate goal, after speaking to Daniel, was to return to fight against the prince of Persia. In addition, the angel gave Daniel a snippet of news about a future event when he informed him the prince of Greece was coming. It was the Babylonians who initially took Daniel captive. Babylon was then overtaken by the Persians, and the next kingdom to rise to world dominion was Greece. These are indisputable historical facts. God's angel, who operated in the spiritual world, wasn't seeing the advancement of the Greek king and his army. He saw the spiritual beings that controlled the Greek king as the force with which he had to contend. Additionally, the angel said his ally was the powerful archangel, Michael. The two last words, "your prince," speak volumes as to where Daniel stood with God. Michael was Daniel's prince! In other words, God assigned Michael to watch over and protect Daniel and the Hebrew people!

We might ask why God allowed Greece to advance and conquer Persia, considering that God's angels were so powerful. Without going into great detail, the short answer is that Michael wasn't assigned to Persia. Remember, Michael had to battle the evil angels assigned to Persia in order for God's message to reach Daniel. The Bible documents the reasons why God permitted kingdoms such as Israel, Judah, Babylon, and Persia to be conquered, and those reasons were always clear and consistent. People always reached a point when their evilness would no longer be tolerated. God not only allowed for their defeat, but He actually drew the opposing king into battle. Why? Because the current ruling nation had surpassed the boundaries God had set against evil and wouldn't allow their actions to go on forever without judgment.

There have been many world empires throughout history. World dominion always emerged when a king became determined and strong enough to take over other kingdoms to build his empire. The strategies used to achieve his objectives were nothing new, as they always included coercion or force. Dominion was always accomplished through acquisition or by force. A kingdom either agreed to fall under the authority of a more powerful ruler or was forced into submission through military action. Nevertheless, submitting to a foreign king meant bondage and loss of personal freedom. The survivors of the defeated kingdom were normally required to pay heavy taxes, become slaves, or in rare cases, be accepted as lesser loyal subjects by agreement.

CHAPTER SIX
If There is a War Between God and Satan, What is the Prize?

We must understand God's desires to more fully comprehend Satan's aspirations. Previously, we read about Satan's ambition. He was an angelic being who wanted his own kingdom, so much so, that he attempted to overpower the throne of his creator. Once thrown from heaven, Satan, along with other defiant angels, continued to fight against God's messenger angels to prevent their communication with humans. This would mean it's extremely important to Satan that people hear him alone. Let's go back to Genesis and take a look at what God wanted for those He created.

> *26 Then God said, "Let us make human beings in our image, to be like us. They will reign over the fish in the sea, the birds in the sky, the livestock, all the wild animals on the earth, and the small animals that scurry along the ground."*
>
> *27 So God created human beings in his own image. In the image of God he created them; male and female he created them.*

[28] Then God blessed them and said, "Be fruitful and multiply. Fill the earth and govern it. Reign over the fish in the sea, the birds in the sky, and all the animals that scurry along the ground." — Genesis 1:26-28

God created man and woman in His own image and blessed them above all His creation. His plan was for humans to have the authority to govern and care for the earth. They were meant to live forever and enjoy loving relationships with Him. It appears that when Satan was thrown down to the earth and its atmosphere, he continued in his quest to reign over all living creatures. However, in order for him to rule, it was necessary to unseat the governorship of humans. Satan executed his strategies to deceive just as he did when he convinced angels to rebel against God. His need to control drove him to manipulate both humans and angels to get them to fall into agreement with him. Satan's character mirrors that of historical and current narcissistic rulers who've had no problem in trampling people in their greed for power and dominion!

According to the Bible, when Adam and Eve chose to believe Satan, they gave him the right to set up his earthly kingdom. He became their accuser before the throne of God as he used their defiance as evidence against them. The following verses were given to the prophet Zechariah in a vision.

> ¹*Then the angel showed me Jeshua the high priest standing before the angel of the* LORD. *The Accuser, Satan, was there at the angel's right hand, making accusations against Jeshua.* ² *And the* LORD *said to Satan, "I, the* LORD, *reject your accusations, Satan. Yes, the* LORD, *who has chosen Jerusalem, rebukes you. This man is like a burning stick that has been snatched from the fire."*
> — Zechariah 3:1-2

Zechariah's vision was of Jeshua, the High Priest, who came obediently before God to intercede for the people. All the while, Satan, the spirit invisible to Jeshua, stood right beside him to argue that he didn't deserve God's blessings. It was God who reprimanded Satan.

Satan had gained many rights forfeited to him by the evil thoughts and deeds of humans; however, because of Abraham's obedience, God made promises to his descendants. He would protect Abraham's descendants in Jerusalem. No matter how evil they became as a people, they would never completely be destroyed. God made promises to Abraham because Abraham chose Him as his God. Abraham's Hebrew descendants were the brand plucked from the fire of Satan's grip. What we may not understand is why God, who commands angels more powerful than Satan and his army, would allow him to execute his reign on earth. The Bible does say that God has a plan to deal with Satan and all evil. It's an eternal and torturous plan. Even the fallen angel, once known as Lucifer, has been given a period of freedom before God judges him for eternity. The Book of

Revelation revealed what his future would be.

> *Then the devil, who had deceived them, was thrown into the fiery lake of burning sulfur, joining the beast and the false prophet. There they will be tormented day and night forever and ever.*
> — Revelation 20:10

Eternity is immeasurable. It means "a time without end." We can hardly comprehend it. We're focused on plans to live our lives as comfortably and fulfilled as possible. Our best hopes are for 70-75, mostly healthy years. Then there's the struggle to maintain our independence through the rest of our lives. After death, we face eternity. The price for evil is extremely severe and unyielding. It would seem God gave mercy to Satan by allowing him to continue to exist in restricted freedom for a determined length of time. To date, that length of time has been for thousands of years. All those years are still a drop in a bucket when compared to eternity. Another interesting thing about God's created beings, is once a spirit has been created, it never dies. The spirit lives forever, somewhere.

Humanity has strived against Satan and his spiritual beings for many generations; however, to God, our lifetime is very short. There's a verse that puts the length of our lives in perspective with that of an eternal God:

> [8] *But you must not forget this one thing, dear friends: A day is like a thousand years to the Lord, and a thousand years is like a day.* — 2 Peter 3:8

The lives of humans are a mere breath in comparison to God's eternal existence. Psalm 78:39 expresses that God realizes this and is merciful.

> *For he remembered that they were merely mortal, gone like a breath of wind that never returns.* — Psalm 78:39

The Book of Revelation has a verse that speaks of the short time Satan's been allowed before he's condemned to his final destination. Also, it reveals how he feels about his fate.

> *[12] Therefore, rejoice, O heavens! And you who live in the heavens, rejoice! But terror will come on the earth and the sea, for the devil has come down to you in great anger, knowing that he has little time."* –– Revelation 12:12

Another verse tells what Satan is doing during the time of his wrath.

> *[8] Stay alert! Watch out for your great enemy, the devil. He prowls around like a roaring lion, looking for someone to devour.* — 1 Peter 5:8

Satan seeks to "devour," which means he seeks to destroy people. He's vengeful, full of hate, murderous, and has an incessant need to separate the created from the creator. Satan, a spiritual being, used his powers to manifest and instill a contrary or opposite reality into human thought. For example, the greatest scientists in the world couldn't argue the intricate complexity of the human body.

Each part and system in the body has been designed for a specific purpose. For example, the respiratory system processes the air we breathe. The circulatory system nourishes every limb with lifeblood. The skeletal system solidifies and stabilizes the body. The nervous system allows for the operation of our senses. The digestive system allows us to intake food, process it, and eliminate wastes in a manner that nourishes the body, but also isolates it from residual contaminants that would cause harm. The reproduction system can be the most intricate system of all. Without it, there would be no human race. Extinction would have occurred with the very first man and woman. The evidence of undeniable order is obvious when we consider the amazing human body.

Satan takes every part of creation and attempts to distort its purpose. His hand is recognizable in the contrary. A body part or system used for a function other than that which it was obviously created, will eventually causes bodily harm. Satan can't change the fact that humans have the ability to think, reason, and choose. He may strategize to deceive us into thinking we have no choices, but Satan's deceptive plans have always been questioned and his control challenged. In his quest for power, he has an incessant need to drive a wedge between humans and their creator, and he will lie, steal, and kill to bring about destruction. He's truly the villain against humanity!

Does God seek the attention of His children?
There were many instances when God communicated to

His people through visions, dreams, and messenger angels. There were also times when God took extreme measures to get the attention of His people. One of the most notorious occasions was when He spoke to Moses through a burning bush.

Many years after Abraham, God called Moses to lead Abraham's descendants out of Egypt, where the Pharaoh held them in slavery for around 400 years. Moses, the son of an Israelite slave, was adopted by the Pharaoh's childless daughter. His upbringing in the palace would suggest he wasn't raised to know the God of Abraham. The Egyptians worshipped the Pharaoh, who in turn acted as the priest to their many gods. As an adult, Moses witnessed an Egyptian soldier beating one of the slaves. An indignant anger rose up inside him, and he killed the soldier. Fearing the Pharaoh's retribution, Moses fled from Egypt. He had been away for forty years when he heard God call him to the mission to free his people.

When God first communicated to Moses, He spoke to him by an angel from within a burning bush. The dry desert bush appeared to be on fire, but didn't burn up. This phenomenon grasped Moses' attention and drew him near. God told Moses to go back to Egypt and free his people so they could return to the land He gave Abraham. This was so God could continue to work through Abraham's descendants to fulfill His promises. Moses knew the slaves in Egypt were well aware that he had been raised in the palace as the Pharaoh's grandson. He couldn't imagine they would listen to him, much less allow him to lead them out of

Egypt. There were well over two million Israelites counting men, women, and children, and moving them would be like moving a small nation. In addition, the exodus from Egypt to their homeland required them to travel through the desert. How would he convince a people of that magnitude to strike out into the desert with their feeble elderly and small children? How would he feed them? How would he get that many people across the Red Sea? It was an overwhelmingly impossible undertaking and an outrageous mission. There was a point while speaking to the burning bush that Moses asked God who would he say sent him.

> [13] *But Moses protested, "If I go to the people of Israel and tell them, 'The God of your ancestors has sent me to you,' they will ask me, 'What is his name?' Then what should I tell them?"*
>
> [14] *God replied to Moses, "I AM WHO I AM. Say this to the people of Israel: I AM has sent me to you."* [15] *God also said to Moses, "Say this to the people of Israel: Yahweh, the God of your ancestors—the God of Abraham, the God of Isaac, and the God of Jacob—has sent me to you. This is my eternal name, my name to remember for all generations.* — Exodus 3:13-15

God's answer to Moses' question was, "I AM WHO I AM." The fascinating thing about this description of Himself was the absolute resolution. It signified that God's character had never, nor would it ever change in the future. Everything He had done or will do defines Him. Though we may rock and sway in our beliefs, opinions, and the stances we take, God's identity is anchored in a depth that's beyond the human understanding. He's an immovable Spirit that doesn't compromise. He would keep His promises because once spoken, they became future reality that wouldn't be denied. His truth was represented by His goodness. Good and evil existed before creation, and God the creator either chose to be good or He was just always good.

Again, if you haven't read about the amazing miracles that transpired to convince the Pharaoh to release the Israelites, I would suggest you read the book of Exodus. The miracles performed also convinced the people they could trust Moses and God's provision. Once released, they began their journey into the desert, where God provided for them and taught them about Himself.

What did God desire to teach the people who chose Him? The Ten Commandments were given to Moses right after he led the Israelites out of Egypt. The first four commandments were about loving and respecting God, and the remaining six taught how to love and respect one another. In the First Commandment, God instructed them to have no other gods before Him. This makes sense because without choosing Him, there would be no reason to adhere to the remaining commandments. The First Commandment establishes an agreement to commit to understanding Him as God and what He wants for His children.

The following were the commandments God gave the people:

> [2] *"I am the LORD your God, who rescued you from the land of Egypt, the place of your slavery.*

> [3] *"You must not have any other god but me.*

> [4] *"You must not make for yourself an idol of any kind or an image of anything in the heavens or on the earth or in the sea.* [5] *You must not bow down to them or worship them, for I, the LORD your God, am a jealous God who will not tolerate your affection for any other gods. I lay the sins of the parents upon their children; the entire family is affected — even children in the third and fourth generations of those who reject me.* [6] *But I lavish unfailing love for a thousand generations on those who love me and obey my commands.*

> [7] *"You must not misuse the name of the LORD your God. The LORD will not let you go unpunished if you misuse his name.*

> [8] *"Remember to observe the Sabbath day by keeping it holy.* [9] *You have six days each week for your ordinary work,* [10] *but the seventh day is a Sabbath day of rest dedicated to the LORD your God. On that day no one in your household may do any work. This includes you, your sons and daughters, your male and female servants, your livestock, and any foreigners living among you.* [11] *For in six days*

IF THERE IS A WAR BETWEEN GOD AND SATAN, WHAT IS THE PRIZE?

the LORD made the heavens, the earth, the sea, and everything in them; but on the seventh day he rested. That is why the LORD blessed the Sabbath day and set it apart as holy.

12 "Honor your father and mother. Then you will live a long, full life in the land the LORD your God is giving you.

13 "You must not murder.

14 "You must not commit adultery.

15 "You must not steal.

16 "You must not testify falsely against your neighbor.

17 "You must not covet your neighbor's house. You must not covet your neighbor's wife, male or female servant, ox or donkey, or anything else that belongs to your neighbor." — Exodus 20:2-17

Undeniably, good and evil are polar opposites. Polar opposite means as far apart as two entities can possibly get. They will never come closer. If it were possible for one to take a step closer, the other would take a step back. God, the creator, set a barrier or boundary against evil. It is God's polar opposite, and it can't exist where He exists. We can only begin to understand God's boundaries by learning more about Him.

So far, we have learned a few things about God. He's the creator. He doesn't force angels or people to accept Him.

His concept of time is hard to imagine. He doesn't want His creation to call anyone or anything God beside Him, and He wants us to be good to each other. Although it may be difficult to understand the complexities of God, it is possible to dig deeper into the characteristics that identify Him.

CHAPTER SEVEN
What Are Other Defining Characteristics of God?

The Bible describes God as good, and He desired to love and do good for His creation. As per His commandments, God expected His children to consider one another before themselves. Just as the golden rule says:

> [12] "Do to others whatever you would like them to do to you. This is the essence of all that is taught in the law and the prophets. — Matthew 7:12

Countless times throughout the Bible, God enticed people to choose to do what was right and good. He continually promised rewards and blessings for those who chose Him and His way. Humanity, for the most part, rejected goodness and honesty and accepted deception, violence, and murder, which ultimately led to the sad state of corruption in which we live today. People have never been inherently prone to do good without selfish motives. Satan may lead humanity to fall to the side of evil, but God's character remained resolute, and He didn't budge an inch to follow. He allowed His creation to go their chosen way, even when those choices led to their own destruction.

Remember the verses we read in the book of Daniel when the messenger angel addressed Daniel as "greatly beloved"? This reveals that an integral part of God's being is love. A verse found in 1 John actually describes God as love.

> *⁸ But anyone who does not love does not know God, for God is love.* – 1 John 4:8

In the Book of Proverbs, there is a declaration and a promise.

> *¹⁷ I love all who love me. Those who search will surely find me.* – Proverbs 8:17

Why would God create humans? Is it possible that somewhere on an infinite timeline, an infinite being decided to create lesser beings so He could share His love? God, who is love, desired to be Father to the children He created, and Satan, who shows no love, desired to steal them away.

Throughout history, people have been greedy, scheming, selfish, manipulative, and murderous, among other loathsome things. How long after the fall of Adam and Eve did it take for someone to commit murder? We have only to look as far as Adam and Eve's children, Cain and Abel, to find the first murder when Cain killed Abel out of a fit of jealousy.

> *⁸ One day Cain suggested to his brother, "Let's go out into the fields." And while they were in the field, Cain attacked his brother, Abel, and killed him.*

52

⁹ Afterward the LORD asked Cain, "Where is your brother? Where is Abel?"

"I don't know," Cain responded. "Am I my brother's guardian?"

¹⁰ But the LORD said, "What have you done? Listen! Your brother's blood cries out to me from the ground! ¹¹ Now you are cursed and banished from the ground, which has swallowed your brother's blood. ¹² No longer will the ground yield good crops for you, no matter how hard you work! From now on you will be a homeless wanderer on the earth."

¹³ Cain replied to the LORD, "My punishment is too great for me to bear! ¹⁴ You have banished me from the land and from your presence; you have made me a homeless wanderer. Anyone who finds me will kill me!"

¹⁵ The LORD replied, "No, for I will give a sevenfold punishment to anyone who kills you." Then the LORD put a mark on Cain to warn anyone who might try to kill him. ¹⁶ So Cain left the LORD's presence and settled in the land of Nod, east of Eden. — Genesis 4:8-16

God judged Cain for his evil act; however, even in that, He showed mercy. God wanted to prevent his children from having blood on their hands should heightened emotions of grief and anger cause them to commit murder.

Obviously, God sets impenetrable boundaries. Satan was barred from heaven; Adam and Eve were barred from the Garden of Eden, and Cain was barred from God's presence.

Behavior, contrary to the goodness of God, produced barriers and drove distance between Him and His creation. With the absence of God's presence, Cain's spiritual guidance became the sole property of Satan. Cain gave Satan that authoritative position through his hatred, envy, and murderous act. With Adam and Eve's son having committed the first murder, Satan's ground game was solidified and in full operation! In God's courtroom, Satan had legally gained the right to continue to empower himself and grow his earthly kingdom as bestowed upon him by those who agreed to do his bidding.

Truth is another foundational characteristic embedded into the very essence of God. Establishing a culture of truth can be an elusive objective. What is truth? Basically, pure truth is the lack of any kind of lie. In our human thinking, we may say, "Wait, there's always room for a place somewhere between," or "There are times when small lies are necessary for a person's well-being." We are human. We sway with the wind and compromise. God, the establisher of truth, doesn't. He doesn't change. He doesn't move. With Him, a thing can't be a little bit true. God's truth is pure and absolute, making it a solid rock on which to stand.

Honestly, the crazy thing about a small lie is that it seems to take on a life of its own and grow. Could it be even the smallest lie is a seed that's sown? The seed meets immediate rejection in God's kingdom and falls into the ground in the kingdom of Satan. Satan then seizes upon his opportunity and quickly assigns a soldier from his army of followers to nurture the seed. Once the seed sprouts, it turns into something far greater and more destructive than was ever intended. The small lie leads to another and ends up amassing into one big destructive lie!

There are many verses that show how important truth is to God.

> *The very essence of your words is truth; all your just regulations will stand forever.* — Psalm 119.160

> *Righteousness and justice are the foundation of your throne. Unfailing love and truth walk before you as attendants.* — Psalm 89:14

> *Truthful words stand the test of time, but lies are soon exposed.* — Proverbs 12:19

> *Yes, truth is gone, and anyone who renounces evil is attacked. The LORD looked and was displeased to find there was no justice.* — Isaiah 59:15

> *"My people bend their tongues like bows to shoot out lies. They refuse to stand up for the truth. They only go from bad to worse. They do not know me,"* says the LORD. — Jeremiah 9:3

We could go on and on with verses written about how important truth is to God, but we get the point. Truth and justice walk hand in hand. There can't be any justice without first having the presence of truth.

We may not fully comprehend the vast array of characteristics that make up the Spirit that is God. However, a broad analysis of the bible, coupled with the humanly impossible fulfillment of thousands of years of prophecies, brings a harmonious insight into the essence of His being. Throughout the Bible, God consistently used the word *Holy* to describe Himself. The biblical context of the word *holy* means set apart. After Moses brought the Jewish slaves out of Egypt, God gave them instructions on how to make everything holy before it came into His presence. This was necessary because He intended to dwell among them. It included their priests, their offering, their temple, themselves, and every item used in their ceremonies. There were many requirements, and when we read them, they seem burdensome. Why was it necessary for everyone and everything that came near God be set apart or made holy?

> [45] *For I, the* LORD, *am the one who brought you up from the land of Egypt, that I might be your God. Therefore, you must be holy because I am holy.*
> — Leviticus 11:45

Holy takes on a broader meaning when speaking of God. Not only does it mean the *setting apart* or *separation of God*, but it also describes Him. God is holy or exalted. He was holy prior to creation. In order for someone to come into His presence, it was necessary they and everything that touched them be made holy. This speaks volumes to the tangent barrier separating good and evil. As a matter of fact, God warned people not to come into His presence without first taking the steps for sanctification. If they were to cross the barrier between good and evil without first cleansing their mind, body, and soul, they would immediately die. The good behind the barrier automatically extinguished the evil in the person. God gave adamant instructions on how to prevent evil from entering too close to His presence for their protection.

What was the purpose of the cleansing steps? The person cleansed himself so he would receive forgiveness for all evil thoughts and deeds. The repentant person was clean for the short period of time that allowed him to go before God. How do we know it was only for a short time? We know because we know human nature. It doesn't take us long to regress and have evil thoughts or do evil deeds. In a fallen world, where the masses turned away from God and toward Satan, God established a way for an obedient group of people to set their hearts right and safely draw as close to Him as possible.

After Moses brought the Israelites out of bondage, he gave them the following before he died:

> *³Indeed, he loves his people; all his holy ones are in his hands. They follow in his steps and accept his teaching.*
>
> *⁴ Moses gave us the Lord's instruction, the special possession of the people of Israel.*

⁵ The LORD became king in Israel—when the leaders of the people assembled, when the tribes of Israel gathered as one." — Deuteronomy 33:3-5

The priests made offerings for the Israelites on the altar of God's temple. The significance of the offering was so the people would understand the severe consequences of evil and receive forgiveness for stepping into its boundaries. The sacrifice represented a substitution for themselves, because the price for doing evil never changed from when Adam and Eve were in the Garden of Eden. It was still death. The people were reminded to turn away from evil for their own protection. When an offering was given with a heart of repentance, the person was restored into right standing with God. God's foremost concern was that truth and sincerity were in their hearts.

Per God's instruction, once a year, the priest was to take two male goats, one for sacrifice and the other released to freedom. The symbolism was the price of death was paid by one of the goats while the other was set free. The freed goat symbolized forgiveness and setting the people free. Along with the sacrifice, the Israelites fasted and reflected on their shortcomings of the past year. Through the process of identifying with the goats, they understood the depth of compassion granted to them before being released from their shame and guilt.

Aaron was Moses' brother, whom God had appointed as the High Priest of the Israelites when they left Egypt. These verses explain what the live goat represented to the people:

> [20] *"When Aaron has finished purifying the Most Holy Place and the Tabernacle and the altar, he must present the live goat.* [21] *He will lay both of his hands on the goat's head and confess over it all the wickedness, rebellion, and sins of the people of Israel. In this way, he will transfer the people's sins to the head of the goat. Then a man specially chosen for the task will drive the goat into the wilderness.* [22] *As the goat goes into the wilderness, it will carry all the people's sins upon itself into a desolate land.* — Leviticus 16:20-22

God wanted those who chose Him to understand the seriousness of the boundary separating Him from evil. Also, He wanted them to understand that within His boundaries, there's a foundation of love, truth, and justice. His intent was for His children to live in peace and harmony. Unfortunately, humanity continued to fail miserably when it came to crossing that boundary between good and evil. God repeatedly extended His mercy and forgiveness to those who would hear Him. The ceremony with the goats symbolized this to the people.

In the beginning, creation was perfect, and Adam and Eve were filled with the love of God. They ate solely from the fruit of the garden God provided. Their love extended to all the animals God gave them for their pleasure. When Adam and Eve believed Satan, the door to knowing evil was opened and could never be shut. God knew the knowledge of evil would cause His children to do evil and it would only increase with time. That fact was painfully clear when Adam and Eve's firstborn, Cain, committed the first murder. Even with this knowledge, God still created humans in His image because He wanted to spend eternity in their presence. God spoke to His heavenly beings concerning the knowledge of evil and its effect on humanity.

> [22] *Then the LORD God said, "Look, the human beings have become like us, knowing both good and evil. What if they reach out, take fruit from the tree of life, and eat it? Then they will live forever!"* [23] *So the LORD God banished them from the Garden of Eden, and he sent Adam out to cultivate the ground from which he had been made.* [24] *After sending them out, the LORD God stationed mighty cherubim to the east of the Garden of Eden. And he placed a flaming sword that flashed back and forth to guard the way to the tree of life.*
> — Genesis 3:22-24

These words only confirm that rampant evil wouldn't be tolerated forever through eternal lives of humans.

After eating the forbidden fruit, the first comprehension Adam and Eve had of their surroundings was the realization they were naked. The new emotion of shame overwhelmed them, so much so, they sewed fig leaves together to cover themselves. Their senses were reacting in an entirely new way to the stimuli of the physical world. Adam, Eve, and all humanity that followed would live in a fallen state until they eventually died. This had to be a harsh and painful reality for them; however, God also suffered because He hadn't created them for this purpose.

One of the harshest realities for Adam and Eve to face had to be that their basic need for covering required a beloved animal be sacrificed. Having never experienced death, their guilt and grief must have overwhelmed them. They would physically see the cost of sin meant death. In addition, their dying bodies would experience hunger and the desire for missing nutrients that they once acquired by merely picking and eating from the garden. God showed mercy by providing covering for them. From that day forward, the first humans, and their families after them, would learn to survive and provide for themselves.

²¹ *And the* LORD *God made clothing from animal skins for Adam and his wife.* — Genesis 3:21

Every time they sacrificed an animal and watched its life-giving blood flow to the ground, Adam and Eve would have remembered their choices were to blame. They couldn't have taken this very lightly, and most likely, they felt both sorrow and repentance. Could the loss of their beloved animals, to meet their needs, have been the very thing that kept Adam and Eve's attitudes humble? Could it be the sacrifice created repentance in their hearts which allowed God to forgive them? This could explain why the sacrifice began and how it was a physical sign of remembrance and realization for the necessity to align their hearts with the heart of God.

We don't really know much about the rest of Adam and Eve's story. Their physical bodies were sentenced to die, but their spirits would live forever, somewhere. It's possible if their hearts remained repentant and humble, they once again found their utopia after their physical death.

Humans obviously began to eat the meat of animals when the garden was no longer available to them. In the centuries to follow, a family's wealth was measured by how much land and livestock they owned. That is, of course, unless they were traders of goods, members of royalty, or worked in the king's government. When Moses led the Hebrew people out of Egypt, God established a system whereby the people could offer the first of their wealth to Him. The offering had to be valuable to the person. It had to be the best of his possessions and cost him something to relinquish. Also, He was expected to give the offering with a willing heart in order for His forgiveness to be pure. Afterward, he walked away with faith, knowing that his relationship with God had been restored. It was the condition of the heart that was most important.

Today, Christians aren't required to sacrifice animals because God always had an alternate solution. He just needed for His children to understand the magnitude of His gift. He would pay the price Himself. We'll talk more about that later, but for now, let's take a look at what the sacrifice was meant to be and what Satan turned it into.

CHAPTER EIGHT
Why Was Blood So Important?

Throughout Biblical history, the day always came when evil inescapably met justice, whether it was the fall of a people, the collapse of a society, or the end of a life. When a life ends, evil is judged and separated from God forever. There was never a possibility for the two to exist together. In His mercy, God provided a way for those who chose Him to restore their relationship. In effect, a person could overcome the imminent, eternal separation that would bind them to evil in its final destination. The physical act of sacrifice represented the spiritual death of evil, but it was worthless if the hearts of the people weren't truly regretful for having committed the things God hated. The sacrifice was a reminder that death and evil were intertwined. God considered life to be in the blood, and death was the loss of life-giving blood. Moses received specific directives from God concerning blood.

> [10] *"And if any native Israelite or foreigner living among you eats or drinks blood in any form, I will turn against that person and cut him off from the*

community of your people, [11] for the life of the body is in its blood. I have given you the blood on the altar to purify you, making you right with the LORD. It is the blood, given in exchange for a life, that makes purification possible. [12] That is why I have said to the people of Israel, 'You must never eat or drink blood—neither you nor the foreigners living among you.' — Leviticus 17:10-12

There's no room for misinterpretation for these verses. Any spiritual practice that includes the consumption of blood never has, nor will it ever be, a directive from God. He further signified the perverseness of drinking blood by commanding a high penalty from anyone who disobeyed. Of course, it's no surprise Satanic worship practices reveled in the drinking of blood. Why? Because Satan was always aware of God's instructions to the people. He knew that by successfully convincing people to do the opposite of God's instruction, he could easily destroy their relationship and ultimately destroy them.

How successful has Satan been in promoting perverse religious rituals?

Shockingly, many of the Israelites eventually agreed to submit to Satan and performed horrendous religious practices. God's commandments to His children were meant to be a protective barrier against the schemes of Satan. However, many disobeyed and co-mingled with the people who lived in the land where God brought them. As generations progressed, they began to participate in worship practices to the Philistine god, Molech. The following verses reveal the people were giving their children to Molech, which triggered an intense rejection from God. Also, we can see what the repulsive act of *giving* their offspring entailed.

> *Then the LORD said to Moses, ² "Give the following instructions to the people of Israel. I am the LORD your God. ³ So do not act like the people in Egypt, where you used to live, or like the people of Canaan, where I am taking you. You must not imitate their way of life.* — Leviticus 18:1-3

> *²¹ And you shall not let any of your descendants pass through the fire to Molech, nor shall you profane the name of your God: I am the LORD.* — Leviticus 18:21 NKJV

> *¹The LORD said to Moses, ² "Give the people of Israel these instructions, which apply both to native Israelites and to the foreigners living in Israel.*

> *"If any of them offer their children as a sacrifice to Molech, they must be put to death. The people of the community must stone them to death. ³ I myself will turn against them and cut them off from the community, because they have defiled my sanctuary and brought shame on my holy name by offering their children to Molech. ⁴ And if the people of the community ignore those who offer their children to Molech and refuse to execute*

*them, ⁵ I myself will turn against them and their
families and will cut them off from the community.
This will happen to all who commit spiritual prostitution by worshiping Molech.*
— Leviticus 20:1-5

The act of giving their children to Molech meant they
took their children to the god's place of worship and
burned them by the fire at his altar. God considered the
murdering of their children to be intolerable, and His warning of retribution was unwaveringly clear.

God also warned the people against consulting mediums and spiritists. Today, we refer to them as fortune
tellers, psychics, mediums, witches, or warlocks, just to
name a few. These people received spiritual advice, but
God assured them it wasn't His advice. God gave messages
to His prophets, but they didn't respond at a person's whim
and certainly not for pay. God expected His children to con-
duct themselves within the boundaries of the instructions
He gave them. The Israelites' interaction with mediums
never led to anything good. They, in effect, submitted to becoming blind puppets with strings controlled by the hand
of Satan as he used the mediums to guide them toward their
destruction.

*⁶ "I will also turn against those who commit spir-
itual prostitution by putting their trust in mediums or in those who consult the spirits of the
dead. I will cut them off from the community. ⁷ So
set yourselves apart to be holy, for I am*

the LORD your God. ⁸ Keep all my decrees by putting them into practice, for I am the LORD who makes you holy. — Leviticus 20:6-8

The following verses in Deuteronomy remind us of what God desired for His children.

¹⁸ *"Appoint judges and officials for yourselves from each of your tribes in all the towns the LORD your God is giving you. They must judge the people fairly. ¹⁹ You must never twist justice or show partiality. Never accept a bribe, for bribes blind the eyes of the wise and corrupt the decisions of the godly. ²⁰ Let true justice prevail, so you may live and occupy the land that the LORD your God is giving you.*

²¹ *"You must never set up a wooden Asherah pole beside the altar you build for the LORD your God. ²² And never set up sacred pillars for worship, for the LORD your God hates them.*
— Deuteronomy 16:18-22

Notice that God commanded, "You shall not plant for yourself an Asherah." What was an Asherah, and why did God hate it? The Philistines worshipped a moon goddess called Ashtoreth, which involved rituals of prostitution. The priests and the people participated in all forms of sexual perversion, and the priests advised the people through divination or fortunetelling. Have you ever heard of an Asherah pole? The worship of this god was its source. The people carved the goddess from the trunk of a tree, basically leaving it without limbs; thus, its identification with a pole. Worship normally took place in a grove of trees during the night because the goddess was considered to be a moon goddess.

Obviously, the worship of Asherah broke the first commandment, which says, "You shall have no gods before me." Sexual rituals included the abuse of the innocent, including children. Once people operated under the influence of Satan, they withheld nothing from themselves as they dwelled on evil continually. Their thoughts became depraved, and they acted out that depravity through their physical bodies.

> ¹*The angel of the* LORD *went up from Gilgal to Bokim and said to the Israelites, "I brought you out of Egypt into this land that I swore to give your ancestors, and I said I would never break my covenant with you.* ² *For your part, you were not to make any covenants with the people living in this land; instead, you were to destroy their altars. But you disobeyed my command. Why did you do this?* ³ *So now I declare that I will no longer drive out the people living in your land. They will be thorns in your sides, and their gods will be a constant temptation to you."*
>
> ⁴ *When the angel of the* LORD *finished speaking to all the Israelites, the people wept loudly.*
> — Judges 2:1-4

Initially, God had promised the land to Abraham's descendants. Abraham and his son Isaac, Isaac's son Jacob, and Jacob's twelve sons were the ancestors of which God spoke. The consequence of dwelling with the Philistines was that they gradually became infiltrated with their evil practices. Without fail, given time and exposure, this always happened. Due to their rejection, God reached a point beyond His tolerance and withdrew His protection against the evil people they chose to follow. Spiritually, the people chose to follow Satan. When the Israelites realized how blinded they had been and the price of their choices, they were distraught. Another consistent thing about God was that He warned many times, but when it was too late, it was too late. When God spoke a word of judgment, that word stood as truth that couldn't be denied. In other words, if the judgment didn't proceed as God spoke it, it would have made God a liar, which was impossible because lying was evil. God wasn't hasty in pronouncing a sentence, and the people understood there was no turning back once the judgment was spoken. In this case, they would live alongside the evil that would eventually turn against them.

The book of Judges was a historical account of the Israelites covering over three hundred years. Before the people demanded a king, God appointed judges to maintain justice. The following verses recount the same story we just read concerning God's decree that the people would dwell with their enemies because they turned to the religions of the land and worshipped the Philistine's moon goddess, Ashtoreth. They also worshipped a god called Baal.

This longer segment found in the book of Judges, chapter 2, gives more insight into what was going on with the people and why they angered God enough to relinquish His protection and give them over to their evil desires. What happens when God becomes so disgusted by evil that He actually causes evil to fall on the people?

> *¹The angel of the LORD went up from Gilgal to Bokim and said to the Israelites, "I brought you out of Egypt into this land that I swore to give your ancestors, and I said I would never break my covenant with you. ² For your part, you were not to make any covenants with the people living in this land; instead, you were to destroy their altars. But you disobeyed my command. Why did you do this? ³ So now I declare that I will no longer drive out the people living in your land. They will be thorns in your sides, and their gods will be a constant temptation to you."*
>
> *⁴ When the angel of the LORD finished speaking to all the Israelites, the people wept loudly. ⁵ So they called the place Bokim (which means "weeping"), and they offered sacrifices there to the LORD.*
>
> *⁶ After Joshua sent the people away, each of the tribes left to take possession of the land allotted to them. ⁷ And the Israelites served the LORD throughout the lifetime of Joshua and the leaders who outlived him—those who had seen all the great things the LORD had done for Israel.*

⁸ Joshua son of Nun, the servant of the LORD, died at the age of 110. ⁹ They buried him in the land he had been allocated, at Timnath-serah in the hill country of Ephraim, north of Mount Gaash.

¹⁰ After that generation died, another generation grew up who did not acknowledge the LORD or remember the mighty things he had done for Israel.

¹¹ The Israelites did evil in the LORD's sight and served the images of Baal. ¹² They abandoned the LORD, the God of their ancestors, who had brought them out of Egypt. They went after other gods, worshiping the gods of the people around them. And they angered the LORD. ¹³ They abandoned the LORD to serve Baal and the images of Ashtoreth. ¹⁴ This made the LORD burn with anger against Israel, so he handed them over to raiders who stole their possessions. He turned them over to their enemies all around, and they were no longer able to resist them. ¹⁵ Every time Israel went out to battle, the LORD fought against them, causing them to be defeated, just as he had warned. And the people were in great distress.

¹⁶ Then the LORD raised up judges to rescue the Israelites from their attackers. ¹⁷ Yet Israel did not listen to the judges but prostituted themselves by worshiping other gods. How quickly they turned away from the path of their ancestors, who had walked in obedience to the LORD's commands.

18 Whenever the LORD raised up a judge over Israel, he was with that judge and rescued the people from their enemies throughout the judge's lifetime. For the LORD took pity on his people, who were burdened by oppression and suffering. 19 But when the judge died, the people returned to their corrupt ways, behaving worse than those who had lived before them. They went after other gods, serving and worshiping them. And they refused to give up their evil practices and stubborn ways.

20 So the LORD burned with anger against Israel. He said, "Because these people have violated my covenant, which I made with their ancestors, and have ignored my commands, 21 I will no longer drive out the nations that Joshua left unconquered when he died. 22 I did this to test Israel—to see whether or not they would follow the ways of the LORD as their ancestors did." 23 That is why the LORD left those nations in place. He did not quickly drive them out or allow Joshua to conquer them all. — Judges 2:1-23

Baal was mentioned in these Bible verses. Who was Baal? Baal was another idol worshipped by the Philistines and other surrounding kingdoms such as Syria. He was depicted as the son of Ashtoreth, the god of storms, as the sea brings different types of storms. He's also been called a god of fertility. Like Asherah, the worship of Baal was riddled with sexual perversion and child sacrifice. The people created his image as a man with an animal head and evil-looking horns. He holds up his right hand with the three middle fingers extended and touching. The thumb pushes the little finger toward the palm. Today, Satanists or Luciferians reveal themselves by using this symbol, among others, while in public. People have become wiser and recognize the symbolism that exposes the Satanists and their evil intentions. The Arch of Baal or the Arch of Palmyra stood at the entrance of the Temple of Baal. It was destroyed by ISIS in Syria in 2015. Archeologists reconstructed it and sent it on a world tour, where it was erected in major cities such as Washington D.C., New York City, London, Dubai, and many others. Spiritually, this structure brings along with it an entourage of territorial demons.

CHAPTER NINE
Is All Hope Lost
When God Has Had Enough?

The Israelites had succumbed to a longstanding, systemic pattern of behavior. If we were to continue to read in Judges, we would learn the cyclical pattern went this way: The people turned away from God and became corrupt; God distanced Himself and ceased to protect them; the people were crushed by the very evil they sought after; the people cried out to God wanting Him to save them; God heard them and restored their relationship. Their conditional relationship was always based on the truth and sincerity in their hearts.

The following verses show that God knew the hearts of people were fickle. The word often used in the Bible was *double-minded*. In other words, the people continued to hang onto things that God hated; therefore, they were never truly sorry for their actions. For that reason, God left tormentors in the land to tempt the Israelites to do evil, just as He left the one tree in the Garden of Eden to tempt Adam and Eve. Everyone was responsible for deciding whether they believed and trusted God.

> [1]These are the nations that the LORD left in the land to test those Israelites who had not experienced the wars of Canaan. [2] He did this to teach warfare to generations of Israelites who had no experience in battle. [3] These are the nations: the Philistines (those living under the five Philistine rulers), all the Canaanites, the Sidonians, and the Hivites living in the mountains of Lebanon from Mount Baal-hermon to Lebo-hamath. [4] These people were left to test the Israelites — to see whether they would obey the commands the LORD had given to their ancestors through Moses.
>
> [5] So the people of Israel lived among the Canaanites, Hittites, Amorites, Perizzites, Hivites, and Jebusites, [6] and they intermarried with them. Israelite sons married their daughters, and Israelite daughters were given in marriage to their sons. And the Israelites served their gods.
>
> [7] The Israelites did evil in the LORD's sight. They forgot about the LORD their God, and they served the images of Baal and the Asherah poles. [8] Then the LORD burned with anger against Israel, and he turned them over to King Cushan-rishathaim of Aram-naharaim. And the Israelites served Cushan-rishathaim for eight years.

> *⁹ But when the people of Israel cried out to the LORD for help, the LORD raised up a rescuer to save them. His name was Othniel, the son of Caleb's younger brother, Kenaz.* — Judges 3:1-9

Over and over again, the pattern repeated as defeats became more devastating and periods of captivity became longer. Eventually, the Israelites were completely banished from the land God had given them. However, God would bring them back, not because they were doing good in His sight, but because God promised they would return and become a nation again. At a future date, a righteous descendant of Abraham would reign forever in Jerusalem, Israel's most holy city.

In the Bible, 1 and 2 Kings gave a historical account of the Israelites. In the following verses, we find Israel had dwindled down to just one tribe, the tribe of Judah. Previously, there had been twelve tribes; each tribe descended from the sons of Jacob.

> *⁷ This disaster came upon the people of Israel because they worshiped other gods. They sinned against the LORD their God, who had brought them safely out of Egypt and had rescued them from the power of Pharaoh, the king of Egypt. ⁸ They had followed the practices of the pagan nations the LORD had driven from the land ahead of them, as well as the practices the kings of Israel had introduced. ⁹ The people of Israel had also secretly done many things that were not pleasing to*

the LORD their God. They built pagan shrines for themselves in all their towns, from the smallest outpost to the largest walled city. ¹⁰ They set up sacred pillars and Asherah poles at the top of every hill and under every green tree. ¹¹ They offered sacrifices on all the hilltops, just like the nations the LORD had driven from the land ahead of them. So the people of Israel had done many evil things, arousing the LORD's anger. ¹² Yes, they worshiped idols, despite the LORD's specific and repeated warnings.

¹³ Again and again the LORD had sent his prophets and seers to warn both Israel and Judah: "Turn from all your evil ways. Obey my commands and decrees—the entire law that I commanded your ancestors to obey, and that I gave you through my servants the prophets."

¹⁴ But the Israelites would not listen. They were as stubborn as their ancestors who had refused to believe in the LORD their God. ¹⁵ They rejected his decrees and the covenant he had made with their ancestors, and they despised all his warnings. They worshiped worthless idols, so they became worthless themselves. They followed the example of the nations around them, disobeying the LORD's command not to imitate them.

¹⁶ They rejected all the commands of the LORD their God and made two calves from metal. They set up

an Asherah pole and worshiped Baal and all the forces of heaven. ¹⁷ They even sacrificed their own sons and daughters in the fire. They consulted fortune-tellers and practiced sorcery and sold themselves to evil, arousing the LORD's anger.

¹⁸ Because the LORD was very angry with Israel, he swept them away from his presence. Only the tribe of Judah remained in the land.
— 2 Kings 17:7-18

Judah was the tribe from which God had promised the righteous king would come. The promise was passed down through Jacob, Abraham's grandson. While Jacob was lying on his deathbed, he gave his last prophecies to his twelve sons. This was what he said to his son, Judah:

⁸ "Judah, your brothers will praise you.
You will grasp your enemies by the neck.
All your relatives will bow before you.
⁹ Judah, my son, is a young lion
that has finished eating its prey.
Like a lion he crouches and lies down;
like a lioness—who dares to rouse him?
¹⁰ The scepter will not depart from Judah,
nor the ruler's staff from his descendants,
until the coming of the one to whom it belongs,
the one whom all nations will honor.
¹¹ He ties his foal to a grapevine,
the colt of his donkey to a choice vine.
He washes his clothes in wine,

his robes in the blood of grapes.
¹² His eyes are darker than wine,
and his teeth are whiter than milk.
—Genesis 49:8-12

In the NKJV Bible, Jacob said the scepter wouldn't depart, "until Shiloh comes." The Hebrew meaning of Shiloh is the *gift from God*. There would be a day when a just and righteous king would reign, and he would be a gift from God.

Around 800 years after Jacob spoke the prophecy to his son Judah, King David carried the promise to future generations. David was thirteen generations from Abraham and ten generations from his ancestor, Judah. God loved David because he continually sought to follow Him. He wasn't perfect and committed some very serious sins, but David was always grieved by them and sought God's forgiveness. In turn, God always forgave him and restored their relationship. The prophet Jeremiah spoke about David's forthcoming descendant.

> ⁵ *"Behold, the days are coming," declares the LORD, "When I will raise up for David a righteous Branch; And He will reign as king and act wisely and do justice and righteousness in the land.*
>
> ⁶ *"In His days Judah will be saved, and Israel will live securely; and this is His name by which He will be called, The LORD Our Righteousness.'*
> —Jeremiah 23:5-6 NASB

Jeremiah prophesied about a future time. The kingdom of Judah eventually separated from the rest of Israel because it became embodied by the evil of its neighbors. Eventually, Israel was conquered by those neighbors. Judah, which included a couple of the remaining tribes, turned back to God under King Hezekiah, almost 250 years after King David's reign.

> ³¹ *When the festival ended, the Israelites who attended went to all the towns of Judah, Benjamin, Ephraim, and Manasseh, and they smashed all the sacred pillars, cut down the Asherah poles, and removed the pagan shrines and altars. After this, the Israelites returned to their own towns and homes.*

> ² *Hezekiah then organized the priests and Levites into divisions to offer the burnt offerings and peace offerings, and to worship and give thanks and praise to the* LORD *at the gates of the Temple.* — 2 Chronicles 31:1-2

> ²⁰ *In this way, King Hezekiah handled the distribution throughout all Judah, doing what was pleasing and good in the sight of the* LORD *his God.* ²¹ *In all that he did in the service of the Temple of God and in his efforts to follow God's laws and commands, Hezekiah sought his God wholeheartedly. As a result, he was very successful.* — 2 Chronicles 31:20-21

The people of Judah, under King Hezekiah, made a choice to follow God. The Kingdom of Judah still remained when Israel was overtaken by its enemies and ceased to be a sovereign nation. Sadly, in just over 100 years, the kings of Judah had reached the end of God's tolerance for evil, and they too suffered the same fate. God sent Jeremiah to Jerusalem to warn the ruler of Judah:

> *²Go out through the Gate of Broken Pots to the garbage dump in the valley of Ben-Hinnom, and give them this message. ³ Say to them, 'Listen to this message from the LORD, you kings of Judah and citizens of Jerusalem! This is what the LORD of Heaven's Armies, the God of Israel, says: I will bring a terrible disaster on this place, and the ears of those who hear about it will ring!*
>
> *⁴ "'For Israel has forsaken me and turned this valley into a place of wickedness. The people burn incense to foreign gods—idols never before acknowledged by this generation, by their ancestors, or by the kings of Judah. And they have filled this place with the blood of innocent children. ⁵ They have built pagan shrines to Baal, and there they burn their sons as sacrifices to Baal. I have never commanded such a horrible deed; it never even crossed my mind to command such a thing! ⁶ So beware, for the time is coming, says the LORD, when this garbage dump will no longer be called Topheth or the valley of Ben-Hinnom, but the Valley of Slaughter. — Jeremiah 19:2-6*

Was there hope for those who believed Jeremiah the prophet?
Once God spoke a judgment, that judgment stood as absolute truth. The Israelites were taken into captivity by the Babylonians. However, God made a provision for those who believed and obeyed what He spoke through the prophet Jeremiah. Jeremiah told the Israelites to submit to captivity, and although they would be under the rulership of a foreign king, they would be allowed to stay and farm their land.

> [9] *"'Do not listen to your false prophets, fortune-tellers, interpreters of dreams, mediums, and sorcerers who say, "The king of Babylon will not conquer you."* [10] *They are all liars, and their lies will lead to your being driven out of your land. I will drive you out and send you far away to die.* [11] *But the people of any nation that submits to the king of Babylon will be allowed to stay in their own country to farm the land as usual. I, the LORD, have spoken!"'* —Jeremiah 27:9-11

Did God stop reaching out to the captives in Babylon?
Jeremiah wasn't taken into captivity, but he continued to give God's message to those who were. He sent a letter to the elders of those who were taken to Babylon.

> *This is what the LORD of Heaven's Armies, the God of Israel, says to all the captives he has exiled to Babylon from Jerusalem:* [5] *"Build homes, and*

plan to stay. Plant gardens, and eat the food they produce. ⁶ Marry and have children. Then find spouses for them so that you may have many grandchildren. Multiply! Do not dwindle away! ⁷ And work for the peace and prosperity of the city where I sent you into exile. Pray to the LORD for it, for its welfare will determine your welfare."

⁸ This is what the LORD of Heaven's Armies, the God of Israel, says: "Do not let your prophets and fortune-tellers who are with you in the land of Babylon trick you. Do not listen to their dreams, ⁹ because they are telling you lies in my name. I have not sent them," says the LORD.

¹⁰ This is what the LORD says: "You will be in Babylon for seventy years. But then I will come and do for you all the good things I have promised, and I will bring you home again. ¹¹ For I know the plans I have for you," says the LORD. "They are plans for good and not for disaster, to give you a future and a hope. ¹² In those days when you pray, I will listen. ¹³ If you look for me wholeheartedly, you will find me. ¹⁴ I will be found by you," says the LORD. "I will end your captivity and restore your fortunes. I will gather you out of the nations where I sent you and will bring you home again to your own land." — Jeremiah 29:4-14

God did exactly that. When the time of His judgment

was over, God put it into the king's heart to relinquish his hold on the Israelites. Not only did He allow them to return to Israel, but He also assisted them by giving provisions.

In addition to Jeremiah's urgent prophecies about the destruction of Judah, he prophesied about a day far in the future when God would once again bring the people back to their homeland. This was to happen after they had been scattered around the world.

> [7] *"Therefore behold, the days are coming," declares the LORD, "when they will no longer say, 'As the LORD lives, who brought up the sons of Israel from the land of Egypt,'* [8] *but, 'As the LORD lives, who brought up and led back the descendants of the household of Israel from the north land and from all the countries where I had driven them.' Then they will live on their own soil."*
> — Jeremiah 23:7-8 NASB

Israel's history has proven the prophecies of Jeremiah, along with the prophecies of many others. Two of those prophets were Isaiah and Ezekiel, and their amazing prophecies can be found in the books of Isaiah and Ezekiel. In 586 B.C., the Kingdom of Judah was overtaken by its enemies. Later, the people were allowed to return to the land and rebuild their temple; however, they remained under the dominion of foreign world powers. They haven't had a king since Judah was overtaken. The prophecies about the coming righteous king are yet to be fulfilled.

The second temple was destroyed by the Romans in 70 A.D., and the people were dispersed as they fled into other nations. In 1948 A.D., through a miraculous turn of events, the Israelites returned to their home, and Israel once again became a nation, just as Jeremiah had prophesied approximately 2500 years earlier.

CHAPTER TEN
What Happened to the Sacrificial System of God?

The sacrificial system, which was for the purpose of receiving forgiveness and restoring relationships to God, ended when the Roman Empire destroyed Jerusalem's Second Temple in 70 A.D. This Temple had been in existence for 420 years. The much grander First Temple was constructed in seven years and stood 419 years from its dedication to its destruction by the Babylonians. For a little perspective as to how much can happen in 400 hundred years, consider that the United States, which began with a meager thirteen colonies, has existed for just 245 years. A lot can change in a much shorter time!

The circumstances surrounding Rome's conquest of Israel, was pretty much the same as prior times, as far as how the people had turned their backs on God. Only this time, the Roman Empire was more brutal, overtaking the people in 63 B.C. and enforcing heavy taxes upon them. Eventually, the Romans destroyed the Second Temple causing the people to flee to the ends of the earth. For almost 2000 years, the Jewish people were in exile from their homeland until 1948 A.D, when once again they returned. Historically, there has never been a nationality of people who have remained intact enough to be restored as a nation after such a long period of time. Their return was the major fulfillment of God's promises through prophecy. The just and righteous king was still to come.

For hundreds of years, Satan desperately sought to destroy the Jewish people in order to prevent the fulfillment of God's promises. He knew the prophecies concerning his final judgment were intertwined with the coming of the Righteous King. Also, prophesied was that Israel would build a Third Temple. Today, there have been major strides in the planning stages for building the temple. Biblical prophecy says the fruition of the Third Temple will enrage Satan and usher him into an attack against the people of Israel. Satan's clash against the Righteous King will end his evil reign of terror.

Later, we'll take a look at what the Bible says about that future event. In order to comprehend what is to take place, it's crucial to know God always promised a substitute for the sacrificial system that ended almost 2000 years ago. Through hundreds of years of prophecy, God promised a righteous king, and He prepared His people to recognize the king's identity. The fulfillment of over 300 humanly impossible prophecies set one man apart. Let's take a look at God's promise and what it entailed.

Who was God's promised righteous king?

Isaiah, who prophesied beginning around 740 B.C., spoke concerning the promised King who would come from a branch of King David. David had died over two hundred years prior to Isaiah's prophesy. The "shoot" would be David's descendant whose lineage came through, Abraham, Isaac, Jacob, and Judah. The prophesied future King would be righteous and fair in His judgments.

> *¹Out of the stump of David's family will grow a shoot—yes, a new Branch bearing fruit from the old root.*
>
> *² And the Spirit of the LORD will rest on him—the Spirit of wisdom and understanding, the Spirit of counsel and might, the Spirit of knowledge and the fear of the LORD.*
>
> *³ He will delight in obeying the LORD. He will not judge by appearance nor make a decision based on hearsay.*
>
> *⁴ He will give justice to the poor and make fair decisions for the exploited. The earth will shake at the force of his word, and one breath from his mouth will destroy the wicked.* — Isaiah 11:1-4

The Old Testament portion of the Bible, which spans approximately 4000 years, makes it painfully obvious that humans have never been capable of consistently doing what was right and just. The Ten Commandments, which were given to Moses, brought conviction, guilt, and shame to the people. They still convict us today. We find it very hard to put strangers before ourselves and our families, and yet, God called for us to love our neighbors as much as we love ourselves. Most people see nothing wrong in lying for self-protection or self-gratification. God saw our human weaknesses and wanted us to realize we would never be guiltless while living in our earthly bodies. Satan, through deception, has worked tirelessly to make sure every person failed and all opportunity to reconcile with our Father is lost.

Apostle Peter gives a clear warning:

> [8]*Stay alert! Watch out for your great enemy, the devil. He prowls around like a roaring lion, looking for someone to devour.* — 1 Peter 5:8

God knew how vulnerable people were when it came to resisting the temptations of Satan, and He didn't turn His back to them? Many Bible verses show that God continually called for people to turn away from evil and toward Him. With long patience, He always kept His door open to those who would return to Him. God has always had a grand plan to defeat Satan and save as many of His children who believed Him. However, true to his character, God's plan would not change the one trait He embedded into the human DNA, and that was everyone still had to make a choice.

What was God's plan?
God had to send His only Son to be the one righteous human. No one else could do it. While on earth, He had to

live a perfect life, without sin, and demonstrate the love of God. Finally, He would be the sacrificial substitution and pay the price of death for everyone who chose to believe God sent Him.

How could God, who is a Spirit, become human? Earlier, we read about instances where God and angels could transform their appearance into human form. This was different. In order for God to come in flesh and blood, God the Spirit had to implant a seed into a human woman. The result was a living, breathing, perfect man who carried the love and power of God while He walked on earth.

Roman's 8:3-4 explains it best:

> [3] *The law of Moses was unable to save us because of the weakness of our sinful nature. So God did what the law could not do. He sent his own Son in a body like the bodies we sinners have. And in that body God declared an end to sin's control over us by giving his Son as a sacrifice for our sins.* [4] *He did this so that the just requirement of the law would be fully satisfied for us, who no longer follow our sinful nature but instead follow the Spirit.*
> — Romans 8:3-4

Who was God's Son?
He was Jesus Christ. How do we know Jesus was the "Messiah" or "anointed one" sent by God? The truth has been substantiated by the vast number of Biblical prophecies foretold the details of the coming Messiah. God began

to refer to His plan early in the book of Genesis after the fall of Adam and Eve. Many Biblical scholars claim that over 400 prophesies, referencing the coming Messiah, were filled by the birth, life, and death of Jesus Christ. The only prophecies left unfulfilled were those about His second coming, which is yet to happen.

There was an in-depth study that gives perspective to the probability of one man fulfilling just EIGHT of the major prophecies about the Messiah. The study was done at Westmont College by Professor Peter Stoner, chairman of the Science Department, in 1958. His mathematical analysis was carefully reviewed and validated by the American Scientific Affiliation. Professor Stoner's results were one in one hundred quadrillion! To give perspective, he explained that if you filled the entire state of Texas with layers of silver dollars up to around knee-high, and put a black checkmark on one coin, and randomly mixed it in. Then blindfold someone and have them pick a coin, and the first coin they pick actually be the one with the black checkmark. That's how easy it would have been for one man to fulfill just eight of the major Biblical prophecies. Jesus fulfilled all eight, plus over 300 more!

Now, you are probably still hung up on the whole idea that God the Spirit could conceive a child through a woman. This wasn't a sexual act, and the woman, Mary, remained a virgin. The seed was planted directly into her womb.

¹⁸*This is how Jesus the Messiah was born. His mother, Mary, was engaged to be married to Joseph. But before the marriage took place, while she was still a virgin, she became pregnant through the power of the Holy Spirit.* ¹⁹*Joseph, to whom she was engaged, was a righteous man and did not want to disgrace her publicly, so he decided to break the engagement quietly.*

²⁰*As he considered this, an angel of the Lord appeared to him in a dream. "Joseph, son of David,"* *the angel said, "do not be afraid to take Mary as your wife. For the child within her was conceived by the Holy Spirit.* ²¹*And she will have a son, and you are to name him Jesus, for he will save his people from their sins."*

²²*All of this occurred to fulfill the Lord's message through his prophet:*

²³*"Look! The virgin will conceive a child!*

She will give birth to a son, and they will call him Immanuel, which means 'God is with us.'"

²⁴*When Joseph woke up, he did as the angel of the Lord commanded and took Mary as his wife.* ²⁵*But he did not have sexual relations with her until her son was born. And Joseph named him Jesus.*
— Matthew 1:18-25

Prior to these verses, the book of Matthew gave the genealogy of Jesus, which brought to light that He descended from King David. Mary's genealogy was also through King David. This was important because the prophecies about the coming Messiah said He would come from that particular genealogy line. God promised Abraham, Isaac, Jacob, Judah, David, and David's son Solomon their descendant, the Righteous King, would reign forever.

Spirits and humans had conceived children prior to the birth of Jesus. These spirits were the fallen angels God created. The angel, Satan, and his army of followers had wreaked havoc on earth. God didn't create angels to procreate with women in a sexual way. He considered it a blasphemous practice. The Satanic/Luciferin worship rituals have always been, and continue to be, sexual in nature as they depict women having sex with male horned demons. We actually see enactments of this on stages as scantily dressed singers and dancers give their cheering audience a taste of Satanic rituals. There have also been many movies about spirits and humans procreating. The Book of Genesis tells just how despicable God found the union of angels and women.

Noah was born about 2000 years after the fall of Adam and Eve. Two thousand years is a very long time, as we saw earlier when comparing to the relatively short time our nation has existed. The world could have changed drastically during that length of time. Again, for perspective, consider the United States is 245 years old as of now. Our country and infrastructure have grown exponentially during an eighth of that time. Also, people lived much longer before the great flood. For example, Noah lived 950 years, Adam lived 930 years, and after the flood, Abraham lived 175 years, and Moses lived 120 years. The world's population could have been much more than it is now and easily have covered the face of the earth!

The people of the earth had become extremely evil. At the time of Noah, as recorded in the book of Genesis chapter six, we can see that angels were mating with women. The result of their union was the birth of giants.

> *¹Then the people began to multiply on the earth, and daughters were born to them. ² The sons of God saw the beautiful women and took any they wanted as their wives. ³ Then the LORD said, "My Spirit will not put up with humans for such a long time, for they are only mortal flesh. In the future, their normal lifespan will be no more than 120 years."*
>
> *⁴ In those days, and for some time after, giant Nephilites lived on the earth, for whenever the sons of God had intercourse with women, they gave birth to children who became the heroes and famous warriors of ancient times.*
>
> *⁵ The LORD observed the extent of human wickedness on the earth, and he saw that everything they thought or imagined was consistently and totally*

evil. ⁶ So the LORD *was sorry he had ever made them and put them on the earth. It broke his heart. ⁷ And the* LORD *said, "I will wipe this human race I have created from the face of the earth. Yes, and I will destroy every living thing— all the people, the large animals, the small animals that scurry along the ground, and even the birds of the sky. I am sorry I ever made them." ⁸ But Noah found favor with the* LORD.
— Genesis 6:1-8

The ungodly bonding of the angels and women created a superhuman race. The evil race was one of mighty giant men, also known as the Nephilim. Unlike the spiritual angels, the giants inhabited a fleshly body that could die; however, their spirits, like all spirits, would never die, nor would they ever enter heaven. The giants had contaminated the blood of the very children God created in his own image. There's a verse in Genesis, chapter six, which has led many to believe Noah was the only man left whose blood wasn't tainted by that of the fallen angels.

⁹This is the genealogy of Noah. Noah was a just man, perfect in his generations. Noah walked with God.—Genesis 6:9 NKJV

We know men weren't perfect in their ways, but this could very well mean that Noah's bloodline maintained its humanity throughout the generations.

In order to preserve His creation, God flooded the earth

to destroy the evil product of the fallen angels. The hearts of people had become so debased that God was sorry He created them. However, being just, He once again proved He would save anyone who chose to deny evil and follow Him. Astonishingly, He found righteousness in only one man, Noah, so God saved him and his family. If Noah hadn't believed God and had faith to build an ark, they too would have perished.

Notice that it was after the flood when God drastically shortened the lifespan of man. Before the flood, men lived to the ripe old age of around 800 years. After the flood, 120 years was about it. Moses was 120 years old when he died. Today, that age is unattainable. Has God found us lacking and shortened our age span once again? It would seem so. Most of us know the rest of the story of Noah and the flood. If not, it can be found in its entirety in Genesis chapters 6, 7, and 8.

Enough about Noah, returning to prophecies about the coming of the Messiah, which means "anointed one" or "chosen one" in Hebrew, the language of the Israelites. The book of Isaiah, chapter 53, written over 400 years before Jesus' birth, prophesied about the Messiah. The following verses tell of His character, how He would be received by the people, and how He would be killed. Also, they tell how His sacrifice gave Him victory over evil.

[1]Who has believed our message

To whom has the LORD revealed his powerful arm?

*² My servant grew up in the L*ORD*'s presence like a tender green shoot, like a root in dry ground.*

There was nothing beautiful or majestic about his appearance, nothing to attract us to him.

³ He was despised and rejected — a man of sorrows, acquainted with deepest grief.

We turned our backs on him and looked the other way. He was despised, and we did not care.

⁴ Yet it was our weaknesses he carried; it was our sorrows that weighed him down.

And we thought his troubles were a punishment from God, a punishment for his own sins!

⁵ But he was pierced for our rebellion, crushed for our sins.

He was beaten so we could be whole. He was whipped so we could be healed.

⁶ All of us, like sheep, have strayed away. We have left God's paths to follow our own.

*Yet the L*ORD *laid on him the sins of us all.*

⁷ He was oppressed and treated harshly, yet he never said a word.

He was led like a lamb to the slaughter.

And as a sheep is silent before the shearers, he did not open his mouth.

⁸ *Unjustly condemned, he was led away.*

No one cared that he died without descendants, that his life was cut short in midstream.

But he was struck down for the rebellion of my people.

⁹ *He had done no wrong and had never deceived anyone.*

But he was buried like a criminal; he was put in a rich man's grave.

¹⁰ *But it was the LORD's good plan to crush him and cause him grief.*

Yet when his life is made an offering for sin, he will have many descendants.

He will enjoy a long life, and the LORD's good plan will prosper in his hands.

¹¹ *When he sees all that is accomplished by his anguish, he will be satisfied.*

And because of his experience, my righteous servant will make it possible for many to be counted righteous, for he will bear all their sins.

¹² *I will give him the honors of a victorious soldier, because he exposed himself to death.*

He was counted among the rebels.

He bore the sins of many and interceded for rebels.
— Isaiah 53

Although fascinating, it's too much for this book to go through all the prophesies Jesus fulfilled as the promised "Messiah." One of the most amazing fulfilled prophecies, was when the foreign world leader, Roman King Caesar Augustus, demanded a census to ensure every nation and people under his control paid taxes. This unprecedented census had to be taken physically, as there were no public birth or death records. Everyone was required to go to their ancestral homes to be manually present for the count. Joseph and a very pregnant Mary had no choice but to leave their home to go to Bethlehem in Judah. This established that they were from the lineage of King David. The precise timing and whim of a foreign ruler was the only thing that caused Joseph to travel with his wife during the late stages of her pregnancy. If they had stayed where they were, Jesus wouldn't have been born in the very tiny city of Bethlehem as foretold by the prophet Micah.

2But you, O Bethlehem Ephrathah, are only a small village among all the people of Judah.

Yet a ruler of Israel, whose origins are in the distant past, will come from you on my behalf.

3 The people of Israel will be abandoned to their enemies until the woman in labor gives birth.

Then at last his fellow countrymen will return from exile to their own land. — Micah 5:2-3

Bethlehem was the birthplace of King David. At a time when there was no king in Israel, and its people were under foreign control, a Roman king's actions established that Jesus was, in fact, David's descendant and further solidified the words of the Prophets. Another fact that limited the probability of Jesus fulfilled the prophecies was that Bethlehem was a very small town.

Now, turning to the life of Jesus, the questions arise, "What did Jesus do while He walked on earth as a man?" "Did He interact with Satan?"

CHAPTER ELEVEN
What Was Jesus' Time on Earth Like?

At the time of Jesus' birth, Caesar Augustus was the emperor of the Roman Empire. It was he who appointed King Herod to rule over Judea, the remainder of the Jewish nation. Herod was an evil, paranoid man hated by the Jewish people. He killed three of his own children, his favorite wife, and multiple relatives because he was afraid they would overpower him and take his kingdom. While lying on his deathbed, he ordered his sister to arrest all the Jewish religious leaders, saying he knew he was dying and no one would mourn his death. He told his sister to kill them when he died to give the people a reason to cry. His sister didn't obey his order; instead, she released them after his death.

The Biblical account of Jesus' birth says when King Herod heard the Messiah had been born, he killed all the male children under the age of two years who lived in the vicinity of Bethlehem. Considering his grievous state of paranoia and willingness to murder his own wife and children to secure his position as king, it seems exactly what he would do. He knew the prophecies concerning the Messiah, who would one day rule as king. In the Book of Matthew, chapter 2, we find the story of how King Herod learned of Jesus' birth and what it meant to the Jewish people.

> *¹Jesus was born in Bethlehem in Judea, during the reign of King Herod. About that time some wise men from eastern lands arrived in Jerusalem, asking, ² "Where is the newborn king of the Jews? We saw his star as it rose, and we have come to worship him."*
>
> *³ King Herod was deeply disturbed when he heard this, as was everyone in Jerusalem. ⁴ He called a meeting of the leading priests and teachers of religious law and asked, "Where is the Messiah supposed to be born?"*
>
> *⁵ "In Bethlehem in Judea," they said, "for this is what the prophet wrote:*
>
> *⁶ 'And you, O Bethlehem in the land of Judah, are not least among the ruling cities of Judah, for a ruler will come from you who will be the shepherd for my people Israel.'"*
>
> *⁷ Then Herod called for a private meeting with the wise men, and he learned from them the time when the star first appeared. ⁸ Then he told them, "Go to Bethlehem and search carefully for the child. And when you find him, come back and tell me so that I can go and worship him, too!"*
>
> *⁹ After this interview the wise men went their way.*

And the star they had seen in the east guided them to Bethlehem. It went ahead of them and stopped over the place where the child was. ¹⁰ When they saw the star, they were filled with joy! ¹¹ They entered the house and saw the child with his mother, Mary, and they bowed down and worshiped him. Then they opened their treasure chests and gave him gifts of gold, frankincense, and myrrh.

¹² When it was time to leave, they returned to their own country by another route, for God had warned them in a dream not to return to Herod.
— Matthew 2:1-12

Of course, King Herod would have had the child killed immediately had the men returned and disclosed His location. Herod's reaction was true to his character.

¹⁶ Herod was furious when he realized that the wise men had outwitted him. He sent soldiers to kill all the boys in and around Bethlehem who were two years old and under, based on the wise men's report of the star's first appearance.

¹⁷ Herod's brutal action fulfilled what God had spoken through the prophet Jeremiah:

¹⁸ "A cry was heard in Ramah—weeping and great mourning. Rachel weeps for her children, refusing to be comforted, for they are dead."
— Mathew 2:16-18

Considering Bethlehem was a very small town with an

approximate population of 1500 people, most likely, King Herod killed fifty or more male toddlers. Satan, the ruler of evil kings, wanted Jesus dead and His mission aborted. King Herod was just a puppet in Satan's evil hands.

God sent an angel to warn Joseph and Mary to leave Bethlehem for Jesus' safety. Joseph fled the country and took his wife and child to Egypt, where they remained until Herod died a few years later.

> [13] *After the wise men were gone, an angel of the Lord appeared to Joseph in a dream. "Get up! Flee to Egypt with the child and his mother," the angel said. "Stay there until I tell you to return, because Herod is going to search for the child to kill him."*
>
> [14] *That night Joseph left for Egypt with the child and Mary, his mother,* [15] *and they stayed there until Herod's death. This fulfilled what the Lord had spoken through the prophet: "I called my Son out of Egypt."* —Matthew 2:13-14

Once again, the actions of an evil king caused the fulfillment of prophecies which identified the child as the Messiah sent by God.

Early in this book, the question was raised in Revelation 12:3-4 as to who was the child that Satan desperately wanted to devour.

> [3] *Then I witnessed in heaven another significant event. I saw a large red dragon with seven heads and ten horns, with seven crowns on his*

heads. ⁴ His tail swept away one-third of the stars in the sky, and he threw them to the earth. He stood in front of the woman as she was about to give birth, ready to devour her baby as soon as it was born. — Revelation 12:3-4

Remember, when reading the Book of Revelation, we have to put on our spiritual eyes to see clearly. The woman represents Israel. Of course, the dragon represents Satan, and the stars are his army of rebellious angels that were thrown out of heaven with him. The child was God's promise to the world. The child would grow, live a perfect life, represent the goodness of God in human form, and finally be the sacrifice that reconciled God's beloved children back to Himself. Through the child, God would sever Satan's control over anyone who chose to believe Him and His plan to save them.

As Jesus grew, He remained hidden until it was time for Him to begin His mission. It had been 400 years since God had given the people a prophet. A man, John the Baptist, had started proclaiming the promised Messiah was alive and walking on earth. People flocked to John to see if he was the one God promised. This was John's message to them:

⁶ God sent a man, John the Baptist, ⁷ to tell about the light so that everyone might believe because of his testimony. ⁸ John himself was not the light; he was simply a witness to tell about the light. ⁹ The one who is the true light, who gives light to everyone, was coming into the world.

¹⁰ He came into the very world he created, but the world didn't recognize him. ¹¹ He came to his own people, and even they rejected him. ¹² But to all who believed him and accepted him, he gave the right to become children of God. ¹³ They are re-born—not with a physical birth resulting from human passion or plan, but a birth that comes from God.

¹⁴ So the Word became human and made his home among us. He was full of unfailing love and faithfulness. And we have seen his glory, the glory of the Father's one and only Son.

¹⁵ John testified about him when he shouted to the crowds, "This is the one I was talking about when I said, 'Someone is coming after me who is far greater than I am, for he existed long before me.'"

¹⁶ From his abundance we have all received one gracious blessing after another. ¹⁷ For the law was given through Moses, but God's unfailing love and faithfulness came through Jesus Christ. ¹⁸ No one has ever seen God. But the unique One, who is himself God, is near to the Father's heart. He has revealed God to us. — John 1:6-18

John was doing a new thing as he prepared the way for the Lord. People flocked to him confessing their sins and asking forgiveness from God. John would then baptize them in the Jordan River. This represented the death and burial of their old self, the washing away of all their evil deeds, and their renewal as in the birth of their new self. John, a prophet, was following instructions from God. He had never met Jesus, but God made a way for him to recognize His Son.

> [13] *Then Jesus went from Galilee to the Jordan River to be baptized by John.* [14] *But John tried to talk him out of it. "I am the one who needs to be baptized by you," he said, "so why are you coming to me?"*
>
> [15] *But Jesus said, "It should be done, for we must carry out all that God requires." So John agreed to baptize him.*
>
> [16] *After his baptism, as Jesus came up out of the water, the heavens were opened and he saw the Spirit of God descending like a dove and settling on him.* [17] *And a voice from heaven said, "This is my dearly loved Son, who brings me great joy."*
> — Matthew 3:13-17

This marked the beginning of Jesus' mission on earth.

Did Jesus confront Satan while on earth?

Yes, He did. If we turn to the Book of Luke, we find an exchange between Jesus and Satan. This confrontation took place immediately after John the Baptist announced Jesus' identity. God allowed Satan to tempt Jesus for forty days in the wilderness. This was to prove the Son of God, in a weak human body, could withstand everything Satan offered where the rest of humanity failed. Even as God's Son, Jesus, had to overcome His bodily pain and deny the temptation to accept the comforts His body craved.

¹Then Jesus, full of the Holy Spirit, returned from the Jordan River. He was led by the Spirit in the wilderness, ²where he was tempted by the devil for forty days. Jesus ate nothing all that time and became very hungry.

³ Then the devil said to him, "If you are the Son of God, tell this stone to become a loaf of bread."

⁴ But Jesus told him, "No! The Scriptures say, 'People do not live by bread alone.'"

⁵ Then the devil took him up and revealed to him all the kingdoms of the world in a moment of time. ⁶ "I will give you the glory of these kingdoms and authority over them," the devil said, "because they are mine to give to anyone I please. ⁷ I will give it all to you if you will worship me."

⁸ Jesus replied, "The Scriptures say, 'You must worship the LORD your God and serve only him.'

⁹ Then the devil took him to Jerusalem, to the highest point of the Temple, and said, "If you are the Son of God, jump off! ¹⁰ For the Scriptures say, 'He will order his angels to protect and guard you.

¹¹ And they will hold you up with their hands so you won't even hurt your foot on a stone.'"

12 Jesus responded, "The Scriptures also say, 'You must not test the LORD your God."

13 When the devil had finished tempting Jesus, he left him until the next opportunity came.
-- Luke 4:1-13

Without a doubt, providing food and water to alleviate hunger and thirst would have been the quickest way for Satan to gain a loyal follower. To win Jesus over, Satan's first attempt was to take advantage of that very basic human need. When Jesus refused to succumb, Satan continued with his routine strategies to satisfy selfishness and greed by offering authority to rule kingdoms. Greed, coupled with the desire for power and fame, had led to the rise and fall of many evil kings and rulers. In exchange for his gifts, Satan required the recipient to worship him. Again, Jesus refused. Clearly, Satan's primary motive was to be like God as he worked diligently to usurp God's place and grow his own earthly kingdom.

An important thing to note, in the exchange between Jesus and Satan, was it was necessary for Satan to gain Jesus' consent in order to make a deal he could act on. This means a person or angel must actively agree to accept Satan's proposal to receive what he offers. His schemes are recognizable by his deceptive and heartless tactics. Getting what we want sounds good, but Satan has never cared who he destroyed in his attempt to control his own destiny. According to the Bible, he doesn't have the power to prevent the judgment that will come upon him and his followers.

He'll never outwit God, nor could he overcome God's mightiest angel, much less His only begotten Son.

Defeated, Satan finally left Jesus, but he wasn't done. He would return and continue his plight to destroy Jesus and God's plan to reconcile His children to Himself. After successfully resisting Satan's temptation, Jesus began His quest to represent His Father by demonstrating the love of God.

Jesus' first action was to choose twelve men to walk alongside Him. He instructed them in the ways of God, and these men became the foundation of His ministry. In the Book of Matthew, chapters 5, 6, and 7, Jesus gave His first sermon called the Sermon on the Mount. It was called this because He went up on a mountain to speak to the people. This long sermon fully revealed the heart of God. The entire speech was lengthy and gave a true understanding of the character of God. I encourage you to go to the Book of Matthew and read it for yourself. The beginning of the sermon has eight guidelines that have been labeled *The Beatitudes*, which means *utmost bliss*. These guidelines are found in chapter 5.

> *¹One day as he saw the crowds gathering, Jesus went up on the mountainside and sat down. His disciples gathered around him, ² and he began to teach them.*

The Beatitudes

[3] *"God blesses those who are poor and realize their need for him, for the Kingdom of Heaven is theirs.*

[4] *God blesses those who mourn, for they will be comforted.*

[5] *God blesses those who are humble, for they will inherit the whole earth.*

[6] *God blesses those who hunger and thirst for justice, for they will be satisfied.*

[7] *God blesses those who are merciful, for they will be shown mercy.*

[8] *God blesses those whose hearts are pure, for they will see God.*

[9] *God blesses those who work for peace, for they will be called the children of God.*

[10] *God blesses those who are persecuted for doing right, for the Kingdom of Heaven is theirs.*
— Matthew 5:1-10

Once again, God's greatest concern was for the good of His children. God is love, and He created humans to love and do good to one another. They were never meant to harm anyone, including themselves, and were always to consider others first. If successful in doing so, God promised He would be their provider, protector, and giver of blessings.

CHAPTER TWELVE
Did Jesus Have Powers?

When it was time for Jesus to reveal Himself, He began to exhibit God's heart for the people by performing healings. As His notoriety spread, He was constantly flocked by crowds. Many examples of the healings He performed are found in the books of Matthew, Luke, Mark, and John.

During that time, one of the most prevalent and feared diseases was leprosy. Leprosy was a contagious, debilitating bacterial disease that ate away the flesh. The blight was recognizable by the appearance of white scaly skin. As the disease progressed, it eventually destroyed the flesh and ate away at the nerves. When someone was found to have the disease, they were immediately banished from society to camps outside of the city. When a leprous person passed someone along the road, they were required to yell, "unclean! unclean!" so the approaching person knew to keep their distance. People were extremely fearful of the leprous disease.

Jesus crossed the boundaries of fear and healed many lepers, even going as far as to touch them. It's unimaginable how the touch of a loving hand must have felt to those who had been so ostracized and isolated. One such healing is found in Matthew chapter eight.

> *¹Large crowds followed Jesus as he came down the mountainside. ² Suddenly, a man with leprosy approached him and knelt before him. "Lord," the man said, "if you are willing, you can heal me and make me clean."*
>
> *³ Jesus reached out and touched him. "I am willing," he said. "Be healed!" And instantly the leprosy disappeared. ⁴ Then Jesus said to him, "Don't tell anyone about this. Instead, go to the priest and let him examine you. Take along the offering required in the law of Moses for those who have been healed of leprosy. This will be a public testimony that you have been cleansed."* — Matthew 8:1-4

On very rare occasions, leprosy diminished, and the person became healed. The Law, given to Moses, required the High Priest to inspect the infected person for signs of the disease. When no sign was present, the priest performed the steps to complete the cleansing. Once finished, the Priest declared them clean, and the once leprous person was reunited with their family and society. When Jesus healed someone, the results were immediate and left no doubt of His miraculous power.

In addition to healing the sick, Jesus raised the dead. One of the most well-known occasions was when Jesus raised Lazarus. Lazarus had been dead for four days and lay in his tomb when Jesus called for him to rise up and come out. The fascinating rendition of the event is well worth taking a couple of minutes to read and can be found in its entirety in John, chapter eleven.

Other miracles included multiplying food. Jesus' first public miracle was to create wine for a wedding celebration after the father of the bride ran out. The father of the bride would have suffered extreme embarrassment for not having the foresight or ability to provide for his daughter's wedding feast. It was Mary, Jesus' mother, who requested the miracle. She obviously knew Jesus was capable of solving the problem, which He did by producing an even higher quality wine. On another occasion, masses of people had followed Jesus for three days as they sought to hear Him speak and to be healed. There were over five thousand very tired and hungry people and no food available. Jesus asked the disciples to search the crowd for food. The only thing they found was five barley loaves and two fish which were brought by a small boy. Jesus took the meager portions and multiplied them into enough food to feed the entire group. After everyone had eaten their fill, the disciples were still able to gather leftover food. Accounts of this event are found in Matthew, Mark, Luke, and John. The book of John, chapter six, has a brief rendition in the first few verses.

What about the demons?

Some of the most remarkable miracles Jesus performed was driving demons out of people. Even young children suffered seriously from demon possession. In biblical times, no one argued or doubted demon possession was a common occurrence. It remains a very real thing today. Jesus taught His disciples how to cast out demons as a vital part of their ministry. Unfortunately, today many say they wholeheartedly believe what has been written in the Bible concerning demon possession; however, compromise with evil has left them ill-equipped to overcome the powers of dark forces or even recognize the source of constant attacks against them their families. Let's read about how Jesus dealt with the demons of Satan's earthly kingdom.

> ³² *That evening after sunset, many sick and demon-possessed people were brought to Jesus.* ³³ *The whole town gathered at the door to watch.* ³⁴ *So Jesus healed many people who were sick with various diseases, and he cast out many demons. But because the demons knew who he was, he did not allow them to speak.* — Mark 1:32-34

Here we see many people came to Jesus because they knew He could heal them and cast out demons. When Jesus began His ministry, it wasn't time for the people to know He was the Son of God. He had to prove Himself to them. The spiritual demons knew exactly who He was. They knew Him long before He came to earth as a man, and they bowed to His authoritative commands when Jesus told them not to speak. Let's take a look at another occasion.

> ³¹ Then Jesus went to Capernaum, a town in Galilee, and taught there in the synagogue every Sabbath day. ³² There, too, the people were amazed at his teaching, for he spoke with authority.
>
> ³³ Once when he was in the synagogue, a man possessed by a demon—an evil spirit—cried out, shouting, ³⁴ "Go away! Why are you interfering with us, Jesus of Nazareth? Have you come to destroy us? I know who you are—the Holy One of God!"
>
> ³⁵ But Jesus reprimanded him. "Be quiet! Come out of the man," he ordered. At that, the demon threw the man to the floor as the crowd watched; then it came out of him without hurting him further.
>
> ³⁶ Amazed, the people exclaimed, "What authority and power this man's words possess! Even evil spirits obey him, and they flee at his command!" ³⁷ The news about Jesus spread through every village in the entire region.
> — Luke 4:31-37

News of Jesus' miraculous healings spread quickly. Soon, His ability to move about freely among the people became greatly inhibited. Another instance happened when Jesus cast demons out of a man who was notorious for his savage strength and frankly for just being completely out of his mind.

26 *So they arrived in the region of the Gerasenes, across the lake from Galilee.* 27 *As Jesus was climbing out of the boat, a man who was possessed by demons came out to meet him. For a long time he had been homeless and naked, living in the tombs outside the town.*

28 *As soon as he saw Jesus, he shrieked and fell down in front of him. Then he screamed, "Why are you interfering with me, Jesus, Son of the Most High God? Please, I beg you, don't torture me!"* 29 *For Jesus had already commanded the evil spirit to come out of him. This spirit had often taken control of the man. Even when he was placed under guard and put in chains and shackles, he simply broke them and rushed out into the wilderness, completely under the demon's power.*

30 *Jesus demanded, "What is your name?"*

"Legion," he replied, for he was filled with many demons. 31 *The demons kept begging Jesus not to send them into the bottomless pit.*

32 *There happened to be a large herd of pigs feeding on the hillside nearby, and the demons begged him to let them enter into the pigs.*

So Jesus gave them permission. 33 *Then the demons came out of the man and entered the pigs, and the entire herd plunged down the steep hillside into the lake and drowned.*

34 When the herdsmen saw it, they fled to the nearby town and the surrounding countryside, spreading the news as they ran. 35 People rushed out to see what had happened. A crowd soon gathered around Jesus, and they saw the man who had been freed from the demons. He was sitting at Jesus' feet, fully clothed and perfectly sane, and they were all afraid. 36 Then those who had seen what happened told the others how the demon-possessed man had been healed. 37 And all the people in the region of the Gerasenes begged Jesus to go away and leave them alone, for a great wave of fear swept over them.

So Jesus returned to the boat and left, crossing back to the other side of the lake. 38 The man who had been freed from the demons begged to go with him. But Jesus sent him home, saying, 39 "No, go back to your family, and tell them everything God has done for you." So he went all through the town proclaiming the great things Jesus had done for him. — Luke 8:26-39

Again, the demons knew exactly who they were speaking to, and their submission to His authority was absolute. Notice they pleaded with Jesus, asking that He wouldn't send them into the abyss. There was no coming back from the abyss; however, by inhabiting the pig's body, they would be free to remain in their territory and search for a new host. It's significant to note it was important for the spiritual demons to have a live fleshly body to possess. When the demons entered the pigs, the pigs lost their collective minds and rushed headlong to their death. Once again, the demons were left without a fleshly host.

We might ask, "Why didn't Jesus just send them to the abyss so they could never enter another person?" The answer is that even evil beings have been given a certain amount of time to exist before God does away with them permanently. They know God has made a declaration of justice for their future and it wasn't time for them to begin serving their sentence. When their time is up, their eternal condemnation begins. Their future punishment will be so severe, God has actually been merciful in allowing them to continue for, what is, by comparison, a very short time.

In this next account, we can see how Jesus' considerable notoriety affected Israel's religious leaders, the Pharisees. They were the priestly sect of Israel. Another priestly sect was the Sadducees. The Pharisees were more concerned about their own prestige, wealth, and maintaining the submissive honor given to them due to their godly positions. These men had become detestable to God, and Jesus reprimanded them often for their evilness.

> [22] *Then a demon-possessed man, who was blind and couldn't speak, was brought to Jesus. He healed the man so that he could both speak and see.* [23] *The crowd was amazed and asked, "Could it be that Jesus is the Son of David, the Messiah?"*

²⁴ But when the Pharisees heard about the miracle, they said, "No wonder he can cast out demons. He gets his power from Satan, the prince of demons."

²⁵ Jesus knew their thoughts and replied, "Any kingdom divided by civil war is doomed. A town or family splintered by feuding will fall apart. ²⁶ And if Satan is casting out Satan, he is divided and fighting against himself. His own kingdom will not survive. ²⁷ And if I am empowered by Satan, what about your own exorcists? They cast out demons, too, so they will condemn you for what you have said. ²⁸ But if I am casting out demons by the Spirit of God, then the Kingdom of God has arrived among you. ²⁹ For who is powerful enough to enter the house of a strong man and plunder his goods? Only someone even stronger—someone who could tie him up and then plunder his house.

³⁰ "Anyone who isn't with me opposes me, and anyone who isn't working with me is actually working against me. — Matthew 12:22-30

The people questioned if Jesus was the Son of David, the promised one who would fulfill the prophecies of their ancestors. The Pharisees were jealous of Jesus. He didn't come to them, nor through their training process. By their reasoning, when the Messiah came, He first would have made himself known to the priests. In their eyes, the one sent by God would surely have honored them just as the people did, and yet, here was an unknown man displaying tremendous powers over sickness and demons. The Pharisees and the Sadducees deemed themselves superior; therefore, they reasoned that Jesus was from Satan. They accused Him of having been sent by Beelzebub, the god worshipped by their enemy, the Philistines. Jesus attempted to reason with them and asked why Satan would diminish his own kingdom through division. Notice Jesus said the priest's sons cast out demons as though it were common knowledge.

Those, who belonged to the priestly tribe of Israel, were meant to walk closely with God and through His anointing, rid the people of torturous demons. It was an everyday part of their obligation to God. Most likely, any success they had was due to God's mercy on the suffering person. Lastly, Jesus reminded them that God gathers people to Himself as opposed to scattering them through division.

In the book of Luke, Jesus explained what happened to an evil spirit after it had been cast out of someone.

> [24] *"When an evil spirit leaves a person, it goes into the desert, searching for rest. But when it finds none, it says, 'I will return to the person I came from.'* [25] *So it returns and finds that its former home is all swept and in order.* [26] *Then the spirit finds seven other spirits more evil than itself, and they all enter the person and live there. And so that person is worse off than before."*
> — Luke 11:24-26

The demon was restless when he no longer dwelled inside a fleshly body. This scripture basically says that once cast out; he wandered around seeking rest in a body he could possess. In his wandering, he found himself in a very dry and uncomfortable situation. Finding no place to inhabit, he decided to go back to the person from which he was cast out. To his delight, he found the person clean and uncluttered, an open space he could occupy. He doesn't have to struggle or fight with other demons in order to take his place. However, this time he decided to strengthen his stronghold on his host by taking a few stronger friends to live with him. Their combined power made it more difficult for anyone to cast them out. Could that person have prevented the re-entry of demon spirits? Yes, he could. Note that neither Jesus nor His disciples feared the demons. Later, we'll read what the Bible says a person can do to protect himself against demons.

When Jesus commanded the demons to come out, they knew exactly who they were confronting, as can be seen in Luke chapter 4:

> *41 Many were possessed by demons; and the demons came out at his command, shouting, "You are the Son of God!" But because they knew he was the Messiah, he rebuked them and refused to let them speak.* — Luke 4:41

Jesus didn't want His identity to be proclaimed to the people by demons. He had a mission, and part of that mission was to show the heart of the Father toward the people through His miraculous healings. Christ wasn't Jesus' last name. *Christ* comes from the Greek word *"christos,"* meaning "the anointed one" or "the chosen one." The Israelite's equivalent Hebrew word was *Messiah.*

The following verses show Jesus gave His disciples the power to do miracles which included healing, casting out demons, and bringing the dead to life again. These were the very same miracles Jesus did while He walked on earth.

> *¹Jesus called his twelve disciples together and gave them authority to cast out evil spirits and to heal every kind of disease and illness.*
>
> *⁷ Go and announce to them that the Kingdom of Heaven is near. ⁸ Heal the sick, raise the dead, cure those with leprosy, and cast out demons. Give as freely as you have received!* — Matthew 10:1, 7-8

Jesus gave the disciples the ability to do the good work of God. The gift to heal and cast out demons was given so they would be successful in presenting the kingdom of heaven. More specifically, they were to present God's love and goodness to the people. The gifts were freely given from God and were never meant to be sold for profit!

How do the demons feel about the human body they so desperately desire to inhabit?

The following story reveals just how much demons hate and wish to destroy the person in whose body they control.

> *¹⁴ And when they had come to the multitude, a man came to Him, kneeling down to Him and say-*

*ing, ¹⁵ "Lord, have mercy on my son, for he is an
epileptic and suffers severely; for he often falls into
the fire and often into the water. ¹⁶ So I brought
him to Your disciples, but they could not cure
him."*

*¹⁷ Then Jesus answered and said, "O faithless
and perverse generation, how long shall I be with
you? How long shall I bear with you? Bring him
here to Me." ¹⁸ And Jesus rebuked the demon, and
it came out of him; and the child was cured from
that very hour.*

*¹⁹ Then the disciples came to Jesus privately and
said, "Why could we not cast it out?"*

*²⁰ So Jesus said to them, "Because of your unbelief;
for assuredly, I say to you, if you have faith as a
mustard seed, you will say to this mountain,
'Move from here to there,' and it will move; and
nothing will be impossible for you. ²¹ However, this
kind does not go out except by prayer and fasting."*
— Matthew 17:14-21 NKJV

There is so much to unwrap here. First, the demon didn't
have a problem with torturing the body in which he re-
sided, and secondly, it's incredibly sad that it's possible for
a demon to possess a child. Jesus taught His disciples it was
their faith that gave them the ability to cast out demons; however, there was a type of demon that was more problem-
atic. In order to win the fight against a stronger demon, they
had to prepare for the confrontation by praying and fasting.

Fasting is denying yourself food, drink, or anything that hinders your time and ability to hear from God about a troubling issue. Fasting enhances a person's ability to focus and seek God's guidance and intervention in a situation. It's important to note it's useless to seek God for anything that goes against His character. It pays to know God. He doesn't help someone to align themselves with the kingdom of Satan.

Early in this book, we read that some angels were more powerful than others. By comparison, it makes sense that some demons would have greater strength and resistance. For this reason, when a person is in the grip of something evil or harmful, the grip is called a *stronghold*. It's also important to remember, it's possible for many demons to possess a person and add strength to their core of resistance.

Here is another example where Jesus healed people possessed by multiple evil spirits:

> [2] *along with some women who had been cured of evil spirits and diseases. Among them were Mary Magdalene, from whom he had cast out seven demons;* — Luke 8:2

Jesus and His disciples successfully drove out evil spirits. They weren't fearful that these demons had any power to enter their bodies and take control. Even though Christians are aware that driving out demons was a crucial part of Jesus' and His disciple's ministry, rarely do they feel confident enough in their faith to demand a demon leave. A significant part of becoming a Christian was to receive the same commission given to the disciples.

CHAPTER THIRTEEN
What Was Jesus' Mission While on Earth?

Since the fall of Adam and Eve in the Garden of Eden, Satan has worked diligently to wreak havoc in the lives of people. Jesus came into the world in human form to destroy the work of Satan.

> *7 Dear children, don't let anyone deceive you about this: When people do what is right, it shows that they are righteous, even as Christ is righteous. 8 But when people keep on sinning, it shows that they belong to the devil, who has been sinning since the beginning. But the Son of God came to destroy the works of the devil.* — 1 John 3:7-8

Satan preyed on humanity and stole the dominion given to them by God, their creator. Jesus came to restore all he had taken. Satan enjoyed an unfair advantage of having the supernatural ability to manifest himself into someone or something he was not. In addition, he possessed age-old knowledge and experience of human behavior, which enabled him to perfect deceptive schemes and produce his desired impact. His schemes were designed to present falsehoods, or evil, in ways that were palatable for people to accept, or at least gradually come to accept. Through his patient deception, he amassed great power and control over the people of the earth.

Did Satan Try to Destroy Jesus' Mission?

In order for Jesus' mission to be successful, the people had to recognize and believe He was the Son of God. For hundreds of years, God sent prophets who foretold of the coming Messiah. The people were to know Him by the fulfillment of those prophecies, the love and truth He exhibited through His teachings, and the miracles He performed. Jesus always guided the people toward the Heavenly Kingdom and their Father. While on earth, He confronted evil boldly and His words and works were for the good of humanity. The religious leaders, Pharisees and Sadducees, were full of corruption that had accumulated over a very long time, and they used their positions to take advantage of the people. Jesus called them out, referring to them as a "brood of snakes":

> [34] *You brood of snakes! How could evil men like you speak what is good and right? For whatever is in your heart determines what you say.* [35] *A good person produces good things from the treasury of a good heart, and an evil person produces evil things from the treasury of an evil heart.*
> — Matthew 12:34-35

Jesus had the ability to know a person's heart, and He knew what was in the hearts of the religious leaders. First, they sought to discredit Jesus by tripping Him up in His words and actions. When that failed, they tried to propa-gandize Him to the people by claiming Satan sent Him, as we read previously. Finally, they simply just sought to kill Him.

Below is an excerpt from the Bible which demonstrates how the religious sect tried to find a reason to discredit Jesus.

> [20] *Watching for their opportunity, the leaders sent spies pretending to be honest men. They tried to get Jesus to say something that could be reported to the Roman governor so he would arrest Jesus.* [21] *"Teacher," they said, "we know that you speak and teach what is right and are not influenced by what others think. You teach the way of God truthfully.* [22] *Now tell us—is it right for us to pay taxes to Caesar or not?"*
>
> [23] *He saw through their trickery and said,* [24] *"Show me a Roman coin. Whose picture and title are stamped on it?"*
>
> *"Caesar's," they replied.*
>
> [25] *"Well then," he said, "give to Caesar what belongs to Caesar, and give to God what belongs to God."*
>
> [26] *So they failed to trap him by what he said in front of the people. Instead, they were amazed by his answer, and they became silent.*
> — Luke 20:20-26

The ruling authority over Israel was the Roman Emperor or Caesar. They believed Jesus would condemn paying taxes to the ungodly Romans who had seized their nation. If they had been successful in tripping Him up in His words, they would have turned Him over to the Roman authorities claiming He was instigating a rebellion against Caesar. Jesus wasn't interested in money and had no time for their trickery. His only interest was the hearts of the people and saving them from Satan.

Another thing that enraged the religious leaders was the parables Jesus told. Parables were short, unrelated stories with double meanings. Through Jesus' parables, they recognized themselves and their own guilt. Their deeds convicted them, and conviction made them extremely angry. One such parable depicted how God had sent many prophets through the years to bring warnings of impending judgment against them if they didn't change their evil ways. The Israelite kings and religious leaders were guilty of imprisoning, beating, and even murdering those prophets in order to prevent the people from hearing God's messages. They had an agenda; it was for the people to do what the religious leaders wanted them to do for the sake of their own continued authority and prosperity.

> *9 Now Jesus turned to the people again and told them this story: "A man planted a vineyard, leased it to tenant farmers, and moved to another country to live for several years. 10 At the time of the grape harvest, he sent one of his servants to collect his*

share of the crop. But the farmers attacked the servant, beat him up, and sent him back empty-handed. ¹¹ So the owner sent another servant, but they also insulted him, beat him up, and sent him away empty-handed. ¹² A third man was sent, and they wounded him and chased him away.

¹³ "'What will I do?' the owner asked himself. 'I know! I'll send my cherished son. Surely they will respect him.'

¹⁴ "But when the tenant farmers saw his son, they said to each other, 'Here comes the heir to this estate. Let's kill him and get the estate for ourselves!' ¹⁵ So they dragged him out of the vineyard and murdered him.

"What do you suppose the owner of the vineyard will do to them?" Jesus asked. ¹⁶ "I'll tell you—he will come and kill those farmers and lease the vineyard to others." "How terrible that such a thing should ever happen," his listeners protested.

¹⁷ Jesus looked at them and said, "Then what does this Scripture mean?

'The stone that the builders rejected has now become the cornerstone.'

¹⁸ Everyone who stumbles over that stone will be broken to pieces, and it will crush anyone it falls on."

19 The teachers of religious law and the leading priests wanted to arrest Jesus immediately because they realized he was telling the story against them—they were the wicked farmers. But they were afraid of the people's reaction. — Luke 20:9-19

On another occasion, the religious leaders invited Jesus to dine with them. Interestingly, they made sure the lawyers were present to try to trip Him up in His words. Not much has changed today! Once again, Jesus took the opportunity to call out their evil behavior.

42 "What sorrow awaits you Pharisees! For you are careful to tithe even the tiniest income from your herb gardens, but you ignore justice and the love of God. You should tithe, yes, but do not neglect the more important things.

43 "What sorrow awaits you Pharisees! For you love to sit in the seats of honor in the synagogues and receive respectful greetings as you walk in the marketplaces. 44 Yes, what sorrow awaits you! For you are like hidden graves in a field. People walk over them without knowing the corruption they are stepping on."

45 "Teacher," said an expert in religious law, "you have insulted us, too, in what you just said."

46 "Yes," said Jesus, "what sorrow also awaits you experts in religious law! For you crush people with unbearable religious demands, and you never lift a finger to ease the burden. ⁴⁷ *What sorrow awaits you! For you build monuments for the prophets your own ancestors killed long ago.* ⁴⁸ *But in fact, you stand as witnesses who agree with what your ancestors did. They killed the prophets, and you join in their crime by building the monuments!* ⁴⁹ *This is what God in his wisdom said about you: 'I will send prophets and apostles to them, but they will kill some and persecute the others.'*

⁵⁰ *"As a result, this generation will be held responsible for the murder of all God's prophets from the creation of the world —* ⁵¹ *from the murder of Abel to the murder of Zechariah, who was killed between the altar and the sanctuary. Yes, it will certainly be charged against this generation.*

⁵² *"What sorrow awaits you experts in religious law! For you remove the key to knowledge from the people. You don't enter the Kingdom yourselves, and you prevent others from entering."*

⁵³ *As Jesus was leaving, the teachers of religious law and the Pharisees became hostile and tried to provoke him with many questions.* ⁵⁴ *They wanted to trap him into saying something they could use against him. —* Luke 11:42-54

One of the Ten Commandments given to Moses, was for the Israelites to keep the *Sabbath day* holy. Basically, this meant God wanted one day a week set aside for His children to rest and spend with Him. If anyone were to break the law of the Sabbath and all it entailed, the religious leaders had the person severely punished. The following story reveals just how debased they had become in their thinking. Strict adherence to their enhanced rules left no room for love or sympathy for the suffering of others.

> *9 Then Jesus went over to their synagogue, 10 where he noticed a man with a deformed hand. The Pharisees asked Jesus, "Does the law permit a person to work by healing on the Sabbath?" (They were hoping he would say yes, so they could bring charges against him.)*
>
> *11 And he answered, "If you had a sheep that fell into a well on the Sabbath, wouldn't you work to pull it out? Of course you would. 12 And how much more valuable is a person than a sheep! Yes, the law permits a person to do good on the Sabbath."*
>
> *13 Then he said to the man, "Hold out your hand." So the man held out his hand, and it was restored, just like the other one! 14 Then the Pharisees called a meeting to plot how to kill Jesus.*
>
> *15 But Jesus knew what they were planning. So he left that area, and many people followed him. He healed all the sick among them,*
> — Matthew 12:9-15

Once again, the hearts of the religious sect were laid bare for the people to witness, as told in this situation where a woman had suffered for eighteen years.

> ¹⁰ One Sabbath day as Jesus was teaching in a synagogue, ¹¹ he saw a woman who had been crippled by an evil spirit. She had been bent double for eighteen years and was unable to stand up straight. ¹² When Jesus saw her, he called her over and said, "Dear woman, you are healed of your sickness!" ¹³ Then he touched her, and instantly she could stand straight. How she praised God!
>
> ¹⁴ But the leader in charge of the synagogue was indignant that Jesus had healed her on the Sabbath day. "There are six days of the week for working," he said to the crowd. "Come on those days to be healed, not on the Sabbath."
>
> ¹⁵ But the Lord replied, "You hypocrites! Each of you works on the Sabbath day! Don't you untie your ox or your donkey from its stall on the Sabbath and lead it out for water? ¹⁶ This dear woman, a daughter of Abraham, has been held in bondage by Satan for eighteen years. Isn't it right that she be released, even on the Sabbath?"
>
> ¹⁷ This shamed his enemies, but all the people rejoiced at the wonderful things he did.
> — Luke 13:10-17

Notice the woman's illness was an affliction by Satan. He had bound her up in this condition for eighteen years.

What better day, than the Lord's Sabbath, to rid a person of a demonic presence?

The price of evil has always been death. The Bible says a day will come when God's tolerance comes to an end, and evil will be judged and separated from good forever. He has the ultimate power to destroy evil and promises He will do just that. God gave laws to Moses, which, if followed, allowed people to continually be reconciled to their creator.

These laws included the sacrifice of animals for the purpose of reminding them the high cost of evil was death. The people were to be grateful for the forgiveness they received and that they weren't paying the price themselves. History has proven the overwhelming majority failed to abide by the laws given by God. God knew this was the consequence of creating a *free will* within His children; however, freedom was necessary for humans to be like Him. God didn't want robots for children. He always had an alternate plan, should His children choose evil, and that plan was to pay the price Himself. God implemented the sacrificial system because He needed people to understand just what allowing Himself to be sacrificed meant for them. In order to receive the gift of reconciliation to God, it was necessary they recognize the anointed one when He came as a man and was sacrificed for all humanity.

How did the sacrifice of Jesus take place?
First, it is important to know God never required the

sacrifice of any human being. Jesus, God's Son, was a part of God who was always with Him during His creation of the heavens and earth. Evil existed, and they knew it would be risky to create humans with the ability to choose between good and evil. When Jesus came in human form, it was with purpose for a mission. Any religion requiring human sacrifice is counterfeit and not of God, but from the king of evil, Satan.

At the religious leaders' demand, the Roman Governor, Pilate, had Jesus beaten and crucified on a cross. The prophet Isaiah foretold of His life and crucifixion approximately 700 years before Jesus' birth.

¹Who has believed our message?

To whom has the LORD revealed his powerful arm?

² My servant grew up in the LORD's presence like a tender green shoot, like a root in dry ground.

There was nothing beautiful or majestic about his appearance, nothing to attract us to him.

³ He was despised and rejected—a man of sorrows, acquainted with deepest grief.

We turned our backs on him and looked the other way. He was despised, and we did not care.

⁴ Yet it was our weaknesses he carried;

it was our sorrows that weighed him down.

And we thought his troubles were a punishment

from God, a punishment for his own sins!

⁵ But he was pierced for our rebellion, crushed for our sins.

He was beaten so we could be whole. He was whipped so we could be healed.

⁶ All of us, like sheep, have strayed away. We have left God's paths to follow our own.

Yet the LORD laid on him the sins of us all.
— Isaiah 53:1-6

There would be nothing about His appearance that would draw people to Him. He would bear the griefs and sorrows of humanity. His body would be pierced through to compensate for sin. He would be scourged so humanity could be healed. All sins were to fall on Him and be sentenced to death. Scourged means whipped. The whip, used by the Romans, was called a 'cat-o'-nine-tails.' Each strip of leather on the whip had pieces of bone or metal at the tips, which lacerated and tore the skin away from the body. The traditional flogging was 39 lashes. Anything beyond was considered a death sentence. Jesus would have received at least 39 lashes.

The prophet, Isaiah, goes on to tell the reason for the sacrifice and what it means to humanity. He also prophesied about the victory that came from the sacrifice.

⁷He was oppressed and treated harshly, yet he never said a word.

He was led like a lamb to the slaughter.

And as a sheep is silent before the shearers, he did not open his mouth.

⁸ Unjustly condemned, he was led away.

No one cared that he died without descendants, that his life was cut short in midstream.

But he was struck down for the rebellion of my people.

⁹ He had done no wrong and had never deceived anyone.

But he was buried like a criminal; he was put in a rich man's grave.

¹⁰ But it was the LORD's good plan to crush him and cause him grief.

Yet when his life is made an offering for sin, he will have many descendants.

He will enjoy a long life, and the LORD's good plan will prosper in his hands.

¹¹ When he sees all that is accomplished by his anguish, he will be satisfied.

And because of his experience, my righteous servant will make it possible for many to be counted righteous, for he will bear all their sins.

¹² I will give him the honors of a victorious soldier, because he exposed himself to death.

He was counted among the rebels.

He bore the sins of many and interceded for rebels.
— Isaiah 53:7-12

Jesus was crucified alongside two thieves. He was treated as a criminal, which meant His body would have been cast aside to be devoured by carnivorous animals or birds. His grave was assigned to be with the wicked, but a rich man named Joseph from Arimathea requested His body and had Him buried in his own tomb. Finally, the Lord was pleased with the success of Jesus' mission because it meant they both would be reunited with the children who chose Him.

The foreign Romans knew nothing about the Jewish prophecies of Isaiah, nor did they have any respect for Jewish laws except to allow them in order to keep peace among the people. They had no idea how their actions toward Jesus were aligning with the hundreds of prophecies about the Messiah. The only alignment they had was with Satan and his intention to kill Jesus. Also, the religious leaders and lawyers had no desire whatsoever to prove Jesus was the *One* sent by God. Their behavior and deeds lined up with and brought about the prophecies which they didn't want to validate. However, their every action did just that.

Let's take a look at how the betrayal and crucifixion of Jesus took place.

CHAPTER FOURTEEN
Who Betrayed and Crucified Jesus?

The Betrayal...
Jesus spoke to His disciples about His death when the time came to finish His mission. Even while Jesus spoke, the enemy plotted for an opportune time to seize Him when He wasn't surrounded by crowds of people.

> [2] *"As you know, Passover begins in two days, and the Son of Man will be handed over to be crucified."*
>
> [3] *At that same time the leading priests and elders were meeting at the residence of Caiaphas, the high priest,* [4] *plotting how to capture Jesus secretly and kill him.* [5] *"But not during the Passover celebration," they agreed, "or the people may riot."*
> — Matthew 26:2-5

I have to comment that these people sound more like politicians than religious leaders, but I digress! It was one in Jesus' close inner circle of twelve disciples who betrayed Him. Jesus always knew this would happen and exactly who the disciple would be. He was Judas Iscariot, the one responsible for taking care of their money.

> [14] *Then Judas Iscariot, one of the twelve disciples, went to the leading priests* [15] *and asked, "How much will you pay me to betray Jesus to you?" And they gave him thirty pieces of silver.* [16] *From that time on, Judas began looking for an opportunity to betray Jesus.* — Matthew 26:14-16

Jesus revealed to His disciples it would be one of them who betrayed Him:

> [20] *When it was evening, Jesus sat down at the table with the Twelve.* [21] *While they were eating, he said, "I tell you the truth, one of you will betray me."*
>
> [22] *Greatly distressed, each one asked in turn, "Am I the one, Lord?"*
>
> [23] *He replied, "One of you who has just eaten from this bowl with me will betray me.* [24] *For the Son of Man must die, as the Scriptures declared long ago. But how terrible it will be for the one who betrays him. It would be far better for that man if he had never been born!"*
>
> [25] *Judas, the one who would betray him, also asked, "Rabbi, am I the one?"*
>
> *And Jesus told him, "You have said it."* — Matthew 26:20-25

After the Passover meal, Jesus went to the Garden of Gethsemane to pray and wait for His betrayer to come. He knew it was time to do what He came to earth to do.

> *36 Then Jesus went with them to the olive grove called Gethsemane, and he said, "Sit here while I go over there to pray." 37 He took Peter and Zebedee's two sons, James and John, and he became anguished and distressed. 38 He told them, "My soul is crushed with grief to the point of death. Stay here and keep watch with me."*
>
> *39 He went on a little farther and bowed with his face to the ground, praying, "My Father! If it is possible, let this cup of suffering be taken away from me. Yet I want your will to be done, not mine."* — Matthew 26:36-39

Judas led the evil mob straight to Jesus, just as was expected.

> *47 And even as Jesus said this, Judas, one of the twelve disciples, arrived with a crowd of men armed with swords and clubs. They had been sent by the leading priests and elders of the people. 48 The traitor, Judas, had given them a prearranged signal: "You will know which one to arrest when I greet him with a kiss." 49 So Judas came straight to Jesus. "Greetings, Rabbi!" he exclaimed and gave him the kiss. 50 Jesus said, "My friend, go ahead and do what you have come for."*

Then the others grabbed Jesus and arrested him. [51] But one of the men with Jesus pulled out his sword and struck the high priest's slave, slashing off his ear. [52] "Put away your sword," Jesus told him. "Those who use the sword will die by the sword. [53] Don't you realize that I could ask my Father for thousands of angels to protect us, and he would send them instantly? [54] But if I did, how would the Scriptures be fulfilled that describe what must happen now?" — Matthew 26:47-54

There were so many humanly impossible Biblical prophecies fulfilled during the time of Jesus' betrayal and crucifixion, even down to the day, on the Passover when it all had to take place. Each prophecy could be a study of its own because of the layers of depth in their meanings. Of course, the Bible tells the events best; however, for this book, we'll focus on some highlights.

Jesus was first taken before the elite of the religious leaders, the High Priest.

[57] Then the people who had arrested Jesus led him to the home of Caiaphas, the high priest, where the teachers of religious law and the elders had gathered. [58] Meanwhile, Peter followed him at a distance and came to the high priest's courtyard. He went in and sat with the guards and waited to see how it would all end.

[59] Inside, the leading priests and the entire high

council were trying to find witnesses who would lie about Jesus, so they could put him to death. [60] But even though they found many who agreed to give false witness, they could not use anyone's testimony. Finally, two men came forward [61] who declared, "This man said, 'I am able to destroy the Temple of God and rebuild it in three days.'"

[62] Then the high priest stood up and said to Jesus, "Well, aren't you going to answer these charges? What do you have to say for yourself?" [63] But Jesus remained silent. Then the high priest said to him, "I demand in the name of the living God—tell us if you are the Messiah, the Son of God."

[64] Jesus replied, "You have said it. And in the future you will see the Son of Man seated in the place of power at God's right hand and coming on the clouds of heaven."

[65] Then the high priest tore his clothing to show his horror and said, "Blasphemy! Why do we need other witnesses? You have all heard his blasphemy. [66] What is your verdict?" "Guilty!" they shouted. "He deserves to die!"

[67] Then they began to spit in Jesus' face and beat him with their fists. And some slapped him, [68] jeering, "Prophesy to us, you Messiah! Who hit you that time?" — Mathew 26:57-68

The betrayal of the Christ, or the Messiah, was prophesied hundreds of years prior by the prophet Jeremiah. Judas' greed was the door that Satan needed to secure his agreement to use him. Satan wanted Jesus dead to prevent Him from carrying out His mission. If Satan could only get the human part of Jesus to fail, he could stop the plan. Once Satan finished using Judas, he left him. This was when Judas came to his senses and realized what he had done.

> [1]*Very early in the morning the leading priests and the elders of the people met again to lay plans for putting Jesus to death.* [2] *Then they bound him, led him away, and took him to Pilate, the Roman governor.*
>
> [3] *When Judas, who had betrayed him, realized that Jesus had been condemned to die, he was filled with remorse. So he took the thirty pieces of silver back to the leading priests and the elders.* [4] *"I have sinned," he declared, "for I have betrayed an innocent man."*
>
> *"What do we care?" they retorted. "That's your problem."*
>
> [5] *Then Judas threw the silver coins down in the Temple and went out and hanged himself.*
>
> [6] *The leading priests picked up the coins. "It wouldn't be right to put this money in the Temple treasury," they said, "since it was payment for murder."* [7] *After some discussion they finally de-*

cided to buy the potter's field, and they made it into a cemetery for foreigners. [8] That is why the field is still called the Field of Blood. [9] This fulfilled the prophecy of Jeremiah that says,

"They took the thirty pieces of silver — the price at which he was valued by the people of Israel, [10] and purchased the potter's field, as the LORD directed."
— Matthew 27:1-10

After a night of interrogation and torture, the religious leaders took Jesus before the Roman government's local authority, Pilate. Their accusations were that Jesus told the Jewish people they should not pay taxes to Caesar; that He claimed to be the Christ, a king; and He had incited people through His teachings. Pilate asked Jesus, "Are you the King of the Jews?" Jesus answered, "It is as you say." Pilate then realized Jesus was from Galilee and unwilling to convict Him; he sent Him to Herod the authority over Jerusalem. (This was not the same Herod who ordered babies killed in Bethlehem when Jesus was born).

Herod was excited to see Jesus because he had heard about the miracles He performed; however, Jesus refused to answer his questions. Herod's soldiers treated Jesus with contempt and mocked him. Finally, Herod had him dressed in a royal robe to mock the Jewish leaders and returned Him to Pilate.

It was customary for Pilate to release a prisoner during the Jewish Passover feast. At the time, the government was holding a despised, notorious murderer named Barabbas. Believing there was no way they would choose to release Barabbas; Pilate gave them a choice between the two of them.

> *¹⁷ As the crowds gathered before Pilate's house that morning, he asked them, "Which one do you want me to release to you—Barabbas, or Jesus who is called the Messiah?" ¹⁸ (He knew very well that the religious leaders had arrested Jesus out of envy.)*
> — Matthew 27:17-18

In their determination to kill Jesus, the religious leaders dug their heels in deeper. The following verses reveal just how desperate they were. Neither Pilate nor Herod found a justifiable reason to kill Jesus. Even Pilate's wife attempted to intervene.

> *⁹ Just then, as Pilate was sitting on the judgment seat, his wife sent him this message: "Leave that innocent man alone. I suffered through a terrible nightmare about him last night."*
>
> *²⁰ Meanwhile, the leading priests and the elders persuaded the crowd to ask for Barabbas to be released and for Jesus to be put to death. ²¹ So the governor asked again, "Which of these two do you want me to release to you?"*
>
> *The crowd shouted back, "Barabbas!"*
>
> *²² Pilate responded, "Then what should I do with Jesus who is called the Messiah?"*

They shouted back, "Crucify him!"

²³ *"Why?" Pilate demanded. "What crime has he committed?"*

But the mob roared even louder, "Crucify him!"

²⁴ *Pilate saw that he wasn't getting anywhere and that a riot was developing. So, he sent for a bowl of water and washed his hands before the crowd, saying, "I am innocent of this man's blood. The responsibility is yours!"*

²⁵ *And all the people yelled back, "We will take responsibility for his death—we and our children!"*

²⁶ *So Pilate released Barabbas to them. He ordered Jesus flogged with a lead-tipped whip, then turned him over to the Roman soldiers to be crucified.* — Matthew 27:19-26

The Crucifixion...

A crucifixion was the Roman way of inflicting one of the most torturous deaths possible upon an individual. Large nails were hammered into the hands and feet to secure the condemned person to a wooden cross. The soldiers then suspended the person in the air for a slow and painful death by asphyxiation. When an authority wanted to rush death, as was with Jesus and the thieves, the soldiers were ordered to break the large femur bone in the legs. In this case, the religious leaders wanted their bodies taken down before the Sabbath, which was the day of rest and a time for them to serve God. It was the day the religious leaders presented sacrifices for the people so they could receive forgiveness for their sins. Jesus was crucified between two thieves. It was the religious leaders who asked that the order be given for the Roman soldiers to break the legs of the three men. When the soldiers came to Jesus, they discovered He had already died and it wasn't necessary to break His legs. All these details, and many more, were prophesied hundreds of years earlier.

The events of Jesus' betrayal and crucifixion are found in the books of Matthew, Luke, Mark, and John. The following portrayal is from the book of John.

> *16 Then Pilate turned Jesus over to them to be crucified.*
>
> *So, they took Jesus away. 17 Carrying the cross by himself, he went to the place called Place of the Skull (in Hebrew, Golgotha). 18 There they nailed him to the cross. Two others were crucified with him, one on either side, with Jesus between them. 19 And Pilate posted a sign on the cross that read, "Jesus of Nazareth, the King of the Jews." 20 The place where Jesus was crucified was near the city, and the sign was written in Hebrew, Latin, and Greek, so that many people could read it.*
>
> *21 Then the leading priests objected and said to Pilate, "Change it from 'The King of the Jews' to 'He said, I am King of the Jews.'"*

²² Pilate replied, "No, what I have written, I have written."

²³ When the soldiers had crucified Jesus, they divided his clothes among the four of them. They also took his robe, but it was seamless, woven in one piece from top to bottom. ²⁴ So they said, "Rather than tearing it apart, let's throw dice for it." This fulfilled the Scripture that says, "They divided my garments among themselves and threw dice for my clothing." So that is what they did.

²⁵ Standing near the cross were Jesus' mother, and his mother's sister, Mary (the wife of Clopas), and Mary Magdalene. ²⁶ When Jesus saw his mother standing there beside the disciple he loved, he said to her, "Dear woman, here is your son." ²⁷ And he said to this disciple, "Here is your mother." And from then on, this disciple took her into his home.

²⁸ Jesus knew that his mission was now finished, and to fulfill Scripture he said, "I am thirsty." ²⁹ A jar of sour wine was sitting there, so they soaked a sponge in it, put it on a hyssop branch, and held it up to his lips. ³⁰ When Jesus had tasted it, he said, "It is finished!" Then he bowed his head and gave up his spirit.

³¹ It was the day of preparation, and the Jewish leaders didn't want the bodies hanging there the next day, which was the Sabbath (and a very special Sabbath, because it was Passover week). So

they asked Pilate to hasten their deaths by ordering that their legs be broken. Then their bodies could be taken down. ³² *So the soldiers came and broke the legs of the two men crucified with Jesus.* ³³ *But when they came to Jesus, they saw that he was already dead, so they didn't break his legs.* ³⁴ *One of the soldiers, however, pierced his side with a spear, and immediately blood and water flowed out.* ³⁵ *(This report is from an eyewitness giving an accurate account. He speaks the truth so that you also may continue to believe.)* ³⁶ *These things happened in fulfillment of the Scriptures that say, "Not one of his bones will be broken,"* ³⁷ *and "They will look on the one they pierced."*

³⁸ *Afterward Joseph of Arimathea, who had been a secret disciple of Jesus (because he feared the Jewish leaders), asked Pilate for permission to take down Jesus' body. When Pilate gave permission, Joseph came and took the body away.* ³⁹ *With him came Nicodemus, the man who had come to Jesus at night. He brought about seventy-five pounds of perfumed ointment made from myrrh and aloes.* ⁴⁰ *Following Jewish burial custom, they wrapped Jesus' body with the spices in long sheets of linen cloth.* ⁴¹ *The place of crucifixion was near a garden, where there was a new tomb, never used before.* ⁴² *And so, because it was the day of preparation for the Jewish Passover and since the tomb was close at hand, they laid Jesus there.*

— John 19:16-42

Jesus said, "It is finished." His mission in a human body was complete, but the reaping of the rewards had just begun. Satan thought he won a great victory when he incited the people against Jesus; instead, he just ushered in a new explosive spiritual power. The death of Jesus' human body was just the beginning.

CHAPTER FIFTEEN
Jesus Was Crucified, Now What?

The book of Matthew details the events that took place immediately upon the death of Jesus and after. When He took His last breath, the earth shook as a new spiritual era was born and darkness lost a major battle.

> *50 Then Jesus shouted out again, and he released his spirit. 51 At that moment the curtain in the sanctuary of the Temple was torn in two, from top to bottom. The earth shook, rocks split apart, 52 and tombs opened. The bodies of many godly men and women who had died were raised from the dead. 53 They left the cemetery after Jesus' resurrection, went into the holy city of Jerusalem, and appeared to many people.*
>
> *54 The Roman officer and the other soldiers at the crucifixion were terrified by the earthquake and all that had happened. They said, "This man truly was the Son of God!"* — Matthew 27:50-54

Only the High Priest could pass through the veil inside the Temple. It marked the entrance of the Holy of Holies, the place where he made sacrifices before the Lord. The sacrifices were to liberate the people from the evil grasp of their sins. If the priest didn't follow God's instructions for cleansing himself of evil before entering into the presence of God, he died. The very presence of God extinguished evil. God's presence had long since left the Temple. That's why the religious leaders had no problem with coming in and out. Their evilness stayed intact because they were never in the presence of God.

The massive veil was amazing in itself. It was as thick as the width of a man's hand (approximately four inches) and was described as sixty feet high, thirty feet wide, and weighed an estimated 8000 lbs. or more. The purpose of the veil was to protect the people from the presence of God. It was a barrier between God and the people that was never to be crossed.

The first thing that happened when Jesus died was the indestructible veil was torn from the top to the bottom. Even if there had been a powerful earthquake, it would have broken the beams holding the veil and left the impossibly massive veil intact. The tearing of the veil was a supernatural, physical sign marking the significance of the spiritual change that occurred at Jesus' death. No longer would there be a barrier between God and the people. No longer would a human priest stand between God and his children. Jesus became the High Priest, and the blood He lost became the spiritual veil or the protective covering which would allow people to enter into the presence of God. Hebrews, chapter 10, makes this clear.

19 And so, dear brothers and sisters, we can boldly enter heaven's Most Holy Place because of the blood of Jesus. 20 By his death, Jesus opened a new and life-giving way through the curtain into the Most Holy Place. 21 And since we have a great High Priest who rules over God's house, 22 let us go right into the presence of God with sincere hearts fully trusting him. For our guilty consciences have been sprinkled with Christ's blood to make us clean, and our bodies have been washed with pure water. — Hebrews 10:19-22

The victory was that Jesus, through His sacrifice, became the good and righteous High Priest. God would never reject His presence when He stood before Him. The people's access to God would never be cut off because of a disqualified evil priest. No longer would there be any further need for an animal sacrifice. During His interrogation by the religious leaders, Jesus told them the next time they saw Him, He would be seated at the right hand of God. It's from that sacred place that Jesus continually intercedes for His people. The new era was described in Romans.

38 And I am convinced that nothing can ever separate us from God's love. Neither death nor life, neither angels nor demons, neither our fears for today nor our worries about tomorrow—not even the powers of hell can separate us from God's love. 39 No power in the sky above or in the earth below—indeed, nothing in all creation will ever be able to separate us from the love of God that is revealed in Christ Jesus our Lord.

— Romans 8:38-39

Now, let's go back to the scene at the cross where Jesus had just died. We read how the rich man, Joseph requested Jesus' body and had Him laid in his own tomb. The religious leaders still had a major concern. They had to make sure the words Jesus had spoken didn't come true.

> *[62] The next day, on the Sabbath, the leading priests and Pharisees went to see Pilate. [63] They told him, "Sir, we remember what that deceiver once said while he was still alive: 'After three days I will rise from the dead.' [64] So we request that you seal the tomb until the third day. This will prevent his disciples from coming and stealing his body and then telling everyone he was raised from the dead! If that happens, we'll be worse off than we were at first."*
>
> *[65] Pilate replied, "Take guards and secure it the best you can." [66] So they sealed the tomb and posted guards to protect it.* — Matthew 27:62-66

Jesus said He would be raised from the dead in three days. Why was His resurrection such an integral part of God's plan?

> *[1]But very early on Sunday morning the women went to the tomb, taking the spices they had prepared. [2] They found that the stone had been rolled*

away from the entrance. ³ So they went in, but they didn't find the body of the Lord Jesus. ⁴ As they stood there puzzled, two men suddenly appeared to them, clothed in dazzling robes.

⁵ The women were terrified and bowed with their faces to the ground. Then the men asked, "Why are you looking among the dead for someone who is alive? ⁶ He isn't here! He is risen from the dead! Remember what he told you

back in Galilee, ⁷ that the Son of Man must be betrayed into the hands of sinful men and be crucified, and that he would rise again on the third day."

⁸ Then they remembered that he had said this. ⁹ So they rushed back from the tomb to tell his eleven disciples—and everyone else—what had happened. — Luke 24:1-9

The disciples, and other followers of Jesus, had fearfully gathered together, believing the Roman soldiers would come for them next. It was there that Jesus appeared to them.

³⁶ And just as they were telling about it, Jesus himself was suddenly standing there among them. "Peace be with you," he said. ³⁷ But the whole group was startled and frightened, thinking they were seeing a ghost!

³⁸ "Why are you frightened?" he asked. "Why are

your hearts filled with doubt? ³⁹ Look at my hands. Look at my feet. You can see that it's really me. Touch me and make sure that I am not a ghost, because ghosts don't have bodies, as you see that I do." ⁴⁰ As he spoke, he showed them his hands and his feet.

⁴¹ Still they stood there in disbelief, filled with joy and wonder. Then he asked them, "Do you have anything here to eat?" ⁴² They gave him a piece of broiled fish, ⁴³ and he ate it as they watched. — Luke 24:36-43

Jesus took great care to prove He stood before them in a human body. He rose from the dead and reminded them He had spoken about His death and resurrection. It wasn't until they encountered a living Jesus that they began to recall the words of the prophets about the Messiah and comprehend what it meant to them.

⁴⁴ Then he said, "When I was with you before, I told you that everything written about me in the law of Moses and the prophets and in the Psalms must be fulfilled." ⁴⁵ Then he opened their minds to understand the Scriptures. ⁴⁶ And he said, "Yes, it was written long ago that the Messiah would suffer and die and rise from the dead on the third day. ⁴⁷ It was also written that this message would be proclaimed in the authority of his name to all the nations, beginning in Jerusalem: 'There is forgiveness of sins for all who repent.' ⁴⁸ You are wit-

nesses of all these things.

⁴⁹ "And now I will send the Holy Spirit, just as my Father promised. But stay here in the city until the Holy Spirit comes and fills you with power from heaven." — Luke 24:44-49

Jesus appeared to the disciples and many others for forty days, teaching about the Kingdom of God. At the end of the forty days, they watched Him ascend into heaven.

¹ In my first book I told you, Theophilus, about everything Jesus began to do and teach ² until the day he was taken up to heaven after giving his chosen apostles further instructions through the Holy Spirit. ³ During the forty days after he suffered and died, he appeared to the apostles from time to time, and he proved to them in many ways that he was actually alive. And he talked to them about the Kingdom of God.

⁴ Once when he was eating with them, he commanded them, "Do not leave Jerusalem until the Father sends you the gift he promised, as I told you before. ⁵ John baptized with water, but in just a few days you will be baptized with the Holy Spirit."

⁶ So when the apostles were with Jesus, they kept asking him, "Lord, has the time come for you to free Israel and restore our kingdom?"

⁷ He replied, "The Father alone has the authority to set those dates and times, and they are not for you to know. ⁸ But you will receive power when the Holy Spirit comes upon you. And you will be my witnesses, telling people about me everywhere—in Jerusalem, throughout Judea, in Samaria, and to the ends of the earth."

⁹ After saying this, he was taken up into a cloud while they were watching, and they could no longer see him. ¹⁰ As they strained to see him rising into heaven, two white-robed men suddenly stood among them. ¹¹ "Men of Galilee," they said, "why are you standing here staring into heaven? Jesus has been taken from you into heaven, but someday he will return from heaven in the same way you saw him go!" — Acts 1:1-11

Who was the "Helper," and why was it so necessary that He come?

Although the disciples didn't fully understand what Jesus was saying while He was with them, when it was time to leave, He told them He would send a "Helper." As a matter of fact, Jesus said the "Helper" could come only after He left.

⁵ "But now I am going away to the one who sent me, and not one of you is asking where I am going. ⁶ Instead, you grieve because of what I've told you. ⁷ But in fact, it is best for you that I go away, because if I don't, the Advocate won't come. If I do go away, then I will send him to you. ⁸ And when he comes, he will convict the world of its sin,

*and of God's righteousness, and of the coming
judgment. ⁹ The world's sin is that it refuses to believe in me. ¹⁰ Righteousness is available because I
go to the Father, and you will see me no
more. ¹¹ Judgment will come because the ruler of
this world has already been judged.* — John 16:5-
11

The Helper brought the understanding of good and evil.
Through his son Jesus, God made His righteous love and
justice known to people. His very goodness exposed the
evil that dwelled in the hearts of humans. God has already
judged the ruler of the world, Satan. Jesus' sacrifice opened
the door for the *Helper* to come live inside of people, where
He strengthened them to stand against the enemy with the
same power Jesus exhibited while on earth. Another name
for the *Helper* is the *Holy Spirit'*. The Holy Spirit was also referred to as the *Spirit of Truth*. There were many times, before
Jesus was born, when God allowed His Spirit to fall on a
person. Most of the time, the Spirit accomplished its purpose and went away. Rarely, did the Spirit dwell with a person. Each time the Spirit fell on someone, He brought
enlightenment, prophesied words of knowledge, answered
to questions, displayed power, or strengthened someone
to carry out missions for the Lord.

It is important to note that spirits are everywhere. Every
created being has a spirit, whether it be the spirit of an
angel, the spirit of a fallen angel, the spirit of a demon, or
the spirit of a human. All are subject to the power of God,

and if God chose to intervene in any given situation to bring about a blessing or a judgment, He could direct any kind of spirit to do His bidding. The spirits, always depicted with a small "s," were those types of spirits. When the Spirit, with a capital "S," was spoken of, it meant the Holy Spirit, the only Spirit who represented God. The Holy Spirit was a part of God, just as Jesus, His son, was a part of Him. Here's a sampling of verses that speak of the Spirit.

> *3 I have filled him with the Spirit of God, giving him great wisdom, ability, and expertise in all kinds of crafts.* — Exodus 31:3

> *24 So Moses went out and reported the LORD's words to the people. He gathered the seventy elders and stationed them around the Tabernacle. 25 And the LORD came down in the cloud and spoke to Moses. Then he gave the seventy elders the same Spirit that was upon Moses. And when the Spirit rested upon them, they prophesied. But this never happened again.* — Numbers 11:24-25

> *10 The Spirit of the LORD came upon him, and he became Israel's judge. He went to war against King Cushan-rishathaim of Aram, and the LORD gave Othniel victory over him.* — Judges 3:10

> *2 The Spirit came into me as he spoke, and he set me on my feet. I listened carefully to his words.* — Ezekiel 2:2

> [14] *I will put my Spirit in you, and you will live again and return home to your own land. Then you will know that I, the* LORD, *have spoken, and I have done what I said. Yes, the* LORD *has spoken!'"* — Ezekiel 37:14

> [8] *But as for me, I am filled with power—with the Spirit of the* LORD. *I am filled with justice and strength to boldly declare Israel's sin and rebellion.* — Micah 3:8

> [20] *Then the Spirit of God came upon Zechariah son of Jehoiada the priest. He stood before the people and said, "This is what God says: Why do you disobey the* LORD's *commands and keep yourselves from prospering? You have abandoned the* LORD, *and now he has abandoned you!"* — 2 Chronicles 24:20

In 1 Samuel, we can see an example of how God brought judgment on the evil choices of a king. The Israelites demanded a king, so God had the prophet Samuel anoint Saul to lead them. In the following verse, God removed His Spirit from Saul because of his evil choices and sent an evil spirit to him instead.

> [14] *Now the Spirit of the* LORD *had left Saul, and the* LORD *sent a tormenting spirit that filled him with depression and fear.* — 1 Samuel 16:14

The prophet, Joel, spoke about the future day when God's Spirit would be poured out on all mankind. Under the power of God's Spirit, there would be prophesying, visions, and dreams.

> ²⁸ *"Then, after doing all those things,*
>
> *I will pour out my Spirit upon all people.*
>
> *Your sons and daughters will prophesy.*
>
> *Your old men will dream dreams,*
>
> *and your young men will see visions.* — Joel 2:28

We already read about how it was the Holy Spirit that God sent to Mary to plant the seed of His son, Jesus.

> ¹⁸ *This is how Jesus the Messiah was born. His mother, Mary, was engaged to be married to Joseph. But before the marriage took place, while she was still a virgin, she became pregnant through the power of the Holy Spirit.* — Matthew 1:18

John the Baptist was the forerunner, or announcer, of the new era that would come through the Messiah, Jesus. John baptized people in water to demonstrate that when someone was forgiven of their sins, it was as though his old self died when submerged in the water. He then rose out of the water, or grave, as a new creation with all sins forgiven. In effect, it represented a new birth, where all sins of the past were washed away and remembered no more. John spoke about his mission:

> ¹¹ *"I baptize with water those who repent of their sins and turn to God. But someone is coming soon who is greater than I am—so much greater that*

I'm not worthy even to be his slave and carry his sandals. He will baptize you with the Holy Spirit and with fire. — Matthew 3:11

At the beginning of His mission, Jesus went to John to be baptized by water. John recognized Him immediately and God confirmed Jesus' identity.

³ Then Jesus went from Galilee to the Jordan River to be baptized by John. ¹⁴ But John tried to talk him out of it. "I am the one who needs to be baptized by you," he said, "so why are you coming to me?"

¹⁵ But Jesus said, "It should be done, for we must carry out all that God requires." So John agreed to baptize him.

¹⁶ After his baptism, as Jesus came up out of the water, the heavens were opened and he saw the Spirit of God descending like a dove and settling on him. ¹⁷ And a voice from heaven said, "This is my dearly loved Son, who brings me great joy."
— Matthew 3:13-17

In the book of John, Jesus told the disciples what they could expect from the Holy Spirit. The Holy Spirit would give them understanding of Jesus' message to them, and He would always glorify Jesus. In turn, Jesus would always glorify the Father. The three were bound as one. How they accomplished their purpose was different, but their message and intent were the same and would always be for the good of humankind, whom they loved.

12 "There is so much more I want to tell you, but you can't bear it now. 13 When the Spirit of truth comes, he will guide you into all truth. He will not speak on his own but will tell you what he has heard. He will tell you about the future. 14 He will bring me glory by telling you whatever he receives from me. 15 All that belongs to the Father is mine; this is why I said, 'The Spirit will tell you whatever he receives from me.' — John 16:12-15

Jesus explained His relationship to the Father and the Holy Spirit before His crucifixion. He told the disciples if they couldn't believe what He said, then believe in His works and the miracles He performed. He also told them one day they would do greater works than He did.

11 Just believe that I am in the Father and the Father is in me. Or at least believe because of the work you have seen me do.

12 "I tell you the truth, anyone who believes in me will do the same works I have done, and even greater works, because I am going to be with the Father. 13 You can ask for anything in my name, and I will do it, so that the Son can bring glory to the Father. 14 Yes, ask me for anything in my name, and I will do it!

15 "If you love me, obey my commandments. 16 And I will ask the Father, and he will give you another Advocate, who will never leave you. 17 He is the

Holy Spirit, who leads into all truth. The world cannot receive him, because it isn't looking for him and doesn't recognize him. But you know him, because he lives with you now and later will be in you. [18] *No, I will not abandon you as orphans—I will come to you.* — John 14:11-18

Now, we have an understanding about the relationship of God, Jesus, and the Holy Spirit, we'll take a look at how the *Helper* arrived to the awaiting disciples after Jesus ascended into heaven.

[1]*On the day of Pentecost all the believers were meeting together in one place.* [2] *Suddenly, there was a sound from heaven like the roaring of a mighty windstorm, and it filled the house where they were sitting.* [3] *Then, what looked like flames or tongues of fire appeared and settled on each of them.* [4] *And everyone present was filled with the Holy Spirit and began speaking in other languages, as the Holy Spirit gave them this ability.*

[5] *At that time there were devout Jews from every nation living in Jerusalem.* [6] *When they heard the loud noise, everyone came running, and they were bewildered to hear their own languages being spoken by the believers.*

[7] *They were completely amazed. "How can this be?" they exclaimed. "These people are all from Galilee,* [8] *and yet we hear them speaking in our*

own native languages! ⁹ Here we are—Parthians, Medes, Elamites, people from Mesopotamia, Judea, Cappadocia, Pontus, the province of Asia, ¹⁰ Phrygia, Pamphylia, Egypt, and the areas of Libya around Cyrene, visitors from Rome ¹¹ (both Jews and converts to Judaism), Cretans, and Arabs. And we all hear these people speaking in our own languages about the wonderful things God has done!" ¹² They stood there amazed and perplexed. "What can this mean?" they asked each other.

¹³ But others in the crowd ridiculed them, saying, "They're just drunk, that's all!" — Acts 2:1-13

What was the Holy Spirit's message to humans?
After the Holy Spirit fell on everyone, Peter, Jesus' disciple stood under the power of the Spirit and preached to the crowds who had gathered on Pentecost. He told the people about Jesus and His mission to set them free. As we just read, his words were heard in every language of those present. Upon hearing Peter's message, conviction struck the hearts of many, and they wanted to receive forgiveness. This is what Peter said to them.

³⁶ "So let everyone in Israel know for certain that God has made this Jesus, whom you crucified, to be both Lord and Messiah!"

³⁷ Peter's words pierced their hearts, and they said to him and to the other apostles, "Brothers, what should we do?"

172

38 Peter replied, "Each of you must repent of your sins and turn to God, and be baptized in the name of Jesus Christ for the forgiveness of your sins. Then you will receive the gift of the Holy Spirit. 39 This promise is to you, to your children, and to those far away—all who have been called by the Lord our God." 40 Then Peter continued preaching for a long time, strongly urging all his listeners, "Save yourselves from this crooked generation!"

41 Those who believed what Peter said were baptized and added to the church that day—about 3,000 in all.

42 All the believers devoted themselves to the apostles' teaching, and to fellowship, and to sharing in meals (including the Lord's Supper), and to prayer.

43 A deep sense of awe came over them all, and the apostles performed many miraculous signs and wonders. — Acts 2:36-43

This was the beginning of Christianity, although it wasn't called Christianity at the time. It began with the Jewish people. Jesus commissioned the disciples to take His simple message throughout the world, and as with all religions, the message has since become more complicated than it was meant to be. This was God's message:

16 "For this is how God loved the world: He

gave his one and only Son, so that everyone who believes in him will not perish but have eternal life. ¹⁷ God sent his Son into the world not to judge the world, but to save the world through him.

¹⁸ *"There is no judgment against anyone who believes in him. But anyone who does not believe in him has already been judged for not believing in God's one and only Son. ¹⁹ And the judgment is based on this fact: God's light came into the world, but people loved the darkness more than the light, for their actions were evil. ²⁰ All who do evil hate the light and refuse to go near it for fear their sins will be exposed. ²¹ But those who do what is right come to the light so others can see that they are doing what God wants."* — John 3:16-21

The open invitation for salvation, meaning to be saved from eternal separation from God, stands until a new era begins. The prophets spoke of the next era, which encompasses the remaining unfulfilled prophecies. It's the time of final judgment and separation of good from evil. This unavoidable time comes when Satan, his demons, and his followers answer for all the evil they inflicted upon God's creation.

CHAPTER SIXTEEN
What Does the Judgment of Evil Encompass?

God has already judged and sentenced evil, and He promised a day when He will carry out Satan's sentence. Evil will no longer be able to tempt or deceive. On that day, all choices will be sealed in heaven and become irrevocable. The spirits of all beings were created to live forever; however, they'll be contained or isolated to a designated eternal dwelling place. The separation of good and evil will be an absolute divide that can't be bridged, as good will no longer be required to tolerate the presence of evil.

Satan won a victory over humanity when he convinced Eve and then Adam to disobey God. His victory allowed him to stand before God in heaven as the accuser of humanity. Why? Because he was right. Although he's evil and had evil intent toward humanity, he told the truth about people, and God honors truth. Early humans agreed to follow Satan and do any evil act he put into their minds. Unfortunately, people have continued to agree with him throughout history.

What did Satan, the accuser of men, want from the righteous judge? He's always wanted the judge, the one with absolute power, to serve justice on people and wipe His hands clean of His creation. In effect, concede His earthly creation over to Satan for his pleasure; frankly, because they belonged together. What would he have said to God all this time? Most likely, "See, they are evil too. They are just like me. They are part of my kingdom, not yours. Stop protecting them and give me complete control." Satan could literally walk away from his session with God, justified in having gained the right to inflict damage upon a person, family, or even a nation.

Job was a good man. In the book of Job, Satan spoke to God about Job:

> *9 Satan replied to the LORD, "Yes, but Job has good reason to fear God. 10 You have always put a wall of protection around him and his home and his property. You have made him prosper in everything he does. Look how rich he is! 11 But reach out and take away everything he has, and he will surely curse you to your face!" — Job 1:9-11*

Job withstood Satan, and his victory was documented as an example for all to read and understand Satan's tactics to inflict devastation on people. Satan knew by turning people against God, they would be bound to him forever.

When Jesus died on the cross and rose again, His victory brought a great war in heaven between God's angels and

Satan and the fallen angels. The accuser, Satan, was displaced as God's Son returned and sat down at His right hand. Through His victory, Jesus became the people's High Priest who would intervene for them continually. He would never be rejected as the intermediary of the people.

> *⁷ Then there was war in heaven. Michael and his angels fought against the dragon and his angels. ⁸ And the dragon lost the battle, and he and his angels were forced out of heaven. ⁹ This great dragon — the ancient serpent called the devil, or Satan, the one deceiving the whole world — was thrown down to the earth with all his angels.*
>
> *¹⁰ Then I heard a loud voice shouting across the heavens, "It has come at last — salvation and power and the Kingdom of our God and the authority of his Christ. For the accuser of our brothers and sisters has been thrown down to earth — the one who accuses them before our God day and night.*
> — Revelation 12:7-10

Jesus overcame, but how are humans supposed to overcome?

John 3:16-21 tells how someone takes advantage of the victory won by Jesus and gets saved from the impending wrath God will eventually inflict on evil.

> *¹⁶ "For this is how God loved the world: He gave his one and only Son, so that everyone who believes in him will not perish but have eternal*

life. 17 God sent his Son into the world not to judge the world, but to save the world through him.

18 "There is no judgment against anyone who believes in him. But anyone who does not believe in him has already been judged for not believing in God's one and only Son. 19 And the judgment is based on this fact: God's light came into the world, but people loved the darkness more than the light, for their actions were evil. 20 All who do evil hate the light and refuse to go near it for fear their sins will be exposed. 21 But those who do what is right come to the light so others can see that they are doing what God wants." — John 3:16-21

Revelation 12 goes on to say this about those who choose to believe and agree with God's plan to save them from being counted as evil in the day of judgment.

11 And they have defeated him by the blood of the Lamb and by their testimony.

And they did not love their lives so much that they were afraid to die.

12 Therefore, rejoice, O heavens!

And you who live in the heavens, rejoice!

But terror will come on the earth and the sea, for the devil has come down to you in great anger, knowing that he has little time."
— Revelation 12:11-12

Salvation, being saved from evil, suddenly became simple. The Israelites received forgiveness when they brought sacrifices to God, along with their grieved hearts for the evil they committed. Now, the High Priest became the eternal sacrifice for everyone. His blood was the only blood that would ever be required. However, to receive the free gift of salvation, it was still necessary to have a sorrowful heart for having committed evil, whether in word, thought, or deed. Obviously, a person had to believe that God sent His Son, Jesus, a part of Himself to be the sacrifice who paid the price for evil. Also, that He rose from the dead and ascended into heaven to sit at the right hand of God, where He acts as an intercessor for all who believe in Him and the sacrifice He made. Lastly, God, who spoke creation into existence, required His children speak their belief in Him and what He did for them. He then sends the *Holy Spirit*, another piece of himself, to dwell inside each person who believes. The Holy Spirit serves as a guide in all things good, as long as He is welcome to do so.

The honor of water baptism demonstrated how the old person was put to death by submerging them into the water, and the new person rises with eternal life to spend with the loving Father and Son.

> [5] *And this hope will not lead to disappointment.*
> *For we know how dearly God loves us, because he*
> *has given us the Holy Spirit to fill our hearts with*
> *his love.* — Romans 5:5

Once cast out of Heaven, Satan was furious. He went from gloating over the death of Jesus and believing he had destroyed the hope of the world, to the realization he was instrumental in initiating the strategic move of God. His personal space got smaller as he was confined to the earth's realm. He was full of hate and revenge. Revelation 12 shows who he focused his anger on.

> [13] When the dragon realized that he had been thrown down to the earth, he pursued the woman who had given birth to the male child. [14] But she was given two wings like those of a great eagle so she could fly to the place prepared for her in the wilderness. There she would be cared for and protected from the dragon for a time, times, and half a time.
>
> [15] Then the dragon tried to drown the woman with a flood of water that flowed from his mouth. [16] But the earth helped her by opening its mouth and swallowing the river that gushed out from the mouth of the dragon. — Revelation 12:13-16

Who was the woman who gave birth to the child? It was the Israelites. Through them, God preserved a pure lineage to give birth to His Son even though there were times His ancestors fell deeply into evil themselves. If not for the promise of Jesus, the Savior, God would have allowed them to fall to the very evil they turned to. Now that all had been accomplished, Satan relentlessly pursued both the Jewish people and the new believers in Christ.

History has confirmed Satan has continually sought to destroy the Jewish people and persecute Christians. He has always turned world leaders against the Jewish people. When, you may ask?

Jesus was crucified around 33 A.D. The Roman Empire sieged Jerusalem and destroyed its Temple in 70 A.D. Christianity had just begun to quickly spread throughout the region. The Romans sought to end it, murdering anywhere from 3000-7000 believers. When the Temple was destroyed, the Jewish people were either murdered or driven out of their nation.

When England came to power, King Edward I issued a decree on July 18, 1290, expelling the Jewish people. When Spain became the world leader, King Ferdinand and Queen Isabella issued a decree against the Jewish people on March 31, 1492, expelling them from Spain. Interestingly, Christopher Columbus sailed from Spain on August 3, 1492. It has been believed that he took many Jews with him, and he may have been Jewish himself. Also fascinating is the Biblical verse:

> *14 But she was given two wings like those of a great eagle so she could fly to the place prepared for her in the wilderness. There she would be cared for and protected from the dragon for a time, times, and half a time. — Revelation 12:14*

Could the two wings of an eagle represent the refuge the Jewish people found in America? America, represented by the eagle, has taken a stand for the defense of Israel.

In the 1930s, the Germans began to persecute the Jewish people, bringing about the Holocaust. In 1948, Israel became a nation again, and the Jewish people began to return to their home, just as the Bible said they would hundreds of years earlier.

How does it end for Satan?
In chapter 20 of Revelation, we find two different endings for the dragon. His first sentence locks him away for 1000 years, and the second locks him away eternally.

> *Then I saw an angel coming down from heaven with the key to the bottomless pit and a heavy chain in his hand. ² He seized the dragon—that old serpent, who is the devil, Satan—and bound him in chains for a thousand years. ³ The angel threw him into the bottomless pit, which he then shut and locked so Satan could not deceive the nations anymore until the thousand years were finished. Afterward he must be released for a little while.*
> — Revelation 20:1-3

The Bible teaches there will be a time when Jesus returns to the earth to reign for a thousand years. Prior to His reign, there's to be a period of great tribulation unlike the world has ever known. A third of the world will be destroyed as evil begins to receive its judgment. God promised He will save those who belong to Him from that tragic time. Jesus taught about His impending return while He was on earth.

29 "Immediately after the anguish of those days, the sun will be darkened, the moon will give no light, the stars will fall from the sky, and the powers in the heavens will be shaken.

30 And then at last, the sign that the Son of Man is coming will appear in the heavens, and there will be deep mourning among all the peoples of the earth. And they will see the Son of Man coming on the clouds of heaven with power and great glory. 31 And he will send out his angels with the mighty blast of a trumpet, and they will gather his chosen ones from all over the world—from the farthest ends of the earth and heaven.

— Matthew 24:29-31

During the thousand years Satan is locked away and the Son of God will reign with absolute truth, fair and equal justice, and irresistible love. Unfortunately, there will be a short period of time, at the end of the thousand years, when everyone living will have to choose between good and evil. Satan will be set free from his prison to tempt and deceive once more. Afterward, he will meet his final and eternal judgment, as found in Revelation 20.

7 When the thousand years come to an end, Satan will be let out of his prison. 8 He will go out to deceive the nations—called Gog and Magog—in every corner of the earth. He will gather them together for battle—a mighty army, as numberless as sand along the seashore. 9 And I saw them as they went up on the broad plain of the earth and surrounded God's people and the beloved city. But fire from heaven came down on the attacking armies and consumed them.

¹⁰ Then the devil, who had deceived them, was thrown into the fiery lake of burning sulfur, joining the beast and the false prophet. There they will be tormented day and night forever and ever. — Revelation 20:7-10

Once Satan has been locked away forever, the final judgment of humans begins. This judgment is for everyone whose names weren't written in the Book of Life. People's lives can be very short. The end and beginning of a new era mean nothing to someone whose life has ended. The opportunity to seal their eternity in heaven ends with the death of the mortal body. Everyone has to decide who they want as their God and they will spend eternity with the God of their choice. Making no choice won't be considered a viable option as a person's thoughts, words, and deeds prove their choice. No matter how good a person may be, they can never measure up to the level required to be in the presence of God. That's only achieved by the protective covering of Jesus' blood.

¹¹ And I saw a great white throne and the one sitting on it. The earth and sky fled from his presence, but they found no place to hide. ¹² I saw the dead, both great and small, standing before God's throne. And the books were opened, including the

*Book of Life. And the dead were judged according
to what they had done, as recorded in the
books. ¹³ The sea gave up its dead, and death and
the grave gave up their dead. And all were judged
according to their deeds. ¹⁴ Then death and the
grave were thrown into the lake of fire. This lake
of fire is the second death. ¹⁵ And anyone whose
name was not found recorded in the Book of Life
was thrown into the lake of fire.* — Revelation
20:11-15

By this time, all that's left are those who chose God. Finally, God will be able to dwell in the presence of his children. All debt to evil will be settled.

*¹ Then I saw a new heaven and a new earth, for the
old heaven and the old earth had disappeared. And
the sea was also gone. ² And I saw the holy city,
the new Jerusalem, coming down from God out of
heaven like a bride beautifully dressed for her hus-
band.*

*³ I heard a loud shout from the throne, saying,
"Look, God's home is now among his people! He
will live with them, and they will be his people.
God himself will be with them. ⁴ He will wipe every
tear from their eyes, and there will be no more
death or sorrow or crying or pain. All these things
are gone forever."*

*⁵ And the one sitting on the throne said, "Look, I
am making everything new!" And then he said to*

me, "Write this down, for what I tell you is trustworthy and true." ⁶ And he also said, "It is finished! I am the Alpha and the Omega—the Beginning and the End. To all who are thirsty I will give freely from the springs of the water of life. ⁷ All who are victorious will inherit all these blessings, and I will be their God, and they will be my children.

⁸ "But cowards, unbelievers, the corrupt, murderers, the immoral, those who practice witchcraft, idol worshipers, and all liars—their fate is in the fiery lake of burning sulfur. This is the second death." — Revelation 21:1-8

The Bible has a promise that Jesus made to those who chose to believe in Him and the mission He completed when He came to earth. The promise is that those who are alive when the great time of tribulation begins will be rescued, if not before, then a least before the worst of it takes place. The tribulation will be a time of pain and suffering like no other. The dead in Christ will rise, and then the living, those who belong to Him will be translated out of the earth and into heaven. This event has been called the *Rapture*, which means *pure joy*.

¹³ And now, dear brothers and sisters, we want you to know what will happen to the believers who have died so you will not grieve like people who have no hope. ¹⁴ For since we believe that Jesus died and was raised to life again, we also believe that when Jesus returns, God will bring back with him the believers who have died.

[15] We tell you this directly from the Lord: We who are still living when the Lord returns will not meet him ahead of those who have died. [16] For the Lord himself will come down from heaven with a commanding shout, with the voice of the archangel, and with the trumpet call of God. First, the believers who have died will rise from their graves. [17] Then, together with them, we who are still alive and remain on the earth will be caught up in the clouds to meet the Lord in the air. Then we will be with the Lord forever. [18] So encourage each other with these words.

— Thessalonians 4:13-18

CHAPTER SEVENTEEN
What Does All This Mean for Mere Humans?

Are they left defenseless against a powerful enemy who's driven by hatred and jealousy? How does someone in a limited mortal body overcome the powerful angel, Satan, and his demons?

Our lives, and our knowledge, are extremely limited compared to that of angelic beings. According to what we've read, demons have the ability to possess people. Humans don't have those kinds of superpowers. Did God, who desired a loving relationship with the children He created, leave them helplessly disadvantaged after the fall of Adam and Eve?

There's a powerful verse in the Bible on which Christians rely and often quote.

> *7 So humble yourselves before God. Resist the devil, and he will flee from you.* — James 4:7

It goes on to say:

> [8] *Come close to God, and God will come close to you. Wash your hands, you sinners; purify your hearts, for your loyalty is divided between God and the world.* — James 4: 8

Frequently, God said if His children would turn to Him, He would protect them. It's impossible to turn to Him without accepting He has spoken the absolute truth. We have to choose Him as our God for Him to be our God. He doesn't drive Satan away from someone who continually invites him to stay.

While on earth, it was well known Jesus had the ability to cast demons out of people. Jesus made it clear humans also took authority over demons, but only if they walked in the authority and power of God.

> [1] *Jesus called his twelve disciples together and gave them authority to cast out evil spirits and to heal every kind of disease and illness.* — Matthew 10:1

> [15] *And then he told them, "Go into all the world and preach the Good News to everyone.* [16] *Anyone who believes and is baptized will be saved. But anyone who refuses to believe will be condemned.* [17] *These miraculous signs will accompany those who believe: They will cast out demons in my name, and they will speak in new languages.* [18] *They will be able to handle snakes with safety, and if they drink anything poisonous, it*

won't hurt them. They will be able to place their hands on the sick, and they will be healed." — Mark 16:15-18

One day Jesus called together his twelve disciples and gave them power and authority to cast out all demons and to heal all diseases. ² Then he sent them out to tell everyone about the Kingdom of God and to heal the sick. — Luke 9:1-2

¹⁶ Then he said to the disciples, "Anyone who accepts your message is also accepting me. And anyone who rejects you is rejecting me. And anyone who rejects me is rejecting God, who sent me."

¹⁷ When the seventy-two disciples returned, they joyfully reported to him, "Lord, even the demons obey us when we use your name!"

¹⁸ "Yes," he told them, "I saw Satan fall from heaven like lightning! ¹⁹ Look, I have given you authority over all the power of the enemy, and you can walk among snakes and scorpions and crush them. Nothing will injure you. ²⁰ But don't rejoice because evil spirits obey you; rejoice because your names are registered in heaven."
— Luke 10:16-20

Jesus gave His disciples the power to drive out demons and do supernatural miracles. The disciples were surprised to find that someone outside of their inner circle was casting out demons under the authority of Jesus' name.

³⁸ John said to Jesus, "Teacher, we saw someone using your name to cast out demons, but we told him to stop because he wasn't in our group."

³⁹ "Don't stop him!" Jesus said. "No one who performs a miracle in my name will soon be able to speak evil of me. ⁴⁰ Anyone who is not against us is for us. ⁴¹ If anyone gives you even a cup of water because you belong to the Messiah, I tell you the truth, that person will surely be rewarded. —
Mark 9:38-41

God wouldn't be mocked. He knew the heart of a person and whether they were a pretender. God wasn't a trick someone could pull out of their hat or something to test or try on. He would never be just 'one of the gods' in a person's repertoire. When a counterfeit person invoked the name of Jesus against a demon, it didn't go very well for them.

¹¹ God gave Paul the power to perform unusual miracles. ¹² When handkerchiefs or aprons that had merely touched his skin were placed on sick people, they were healed of their diseases, and evil spirits were expelled.

¹³ A group of Jews was traveling from town to town casting out evil spirits. They tried to use the name of the Lord Jesus in their incantation, saying, "I command you in the name of Jesus, whom Paul preaches, to come out!" ¹⁴ Seven sons of

Sceva, a leading priest, were doing this. [15] *But one time when they tried it, the evil spirit replied, "I know Jesus, and I know Paul, but who are you?"* [16] *Then the man with the evil spirit leaped on them, overpowered them, and attacked them with such violence that they fled from the house, naked and battered.*

[17] *The story of what happened spread quickly all through Ephesus, to Jews and Greeks alike. A solemn fear descended on the city, and the name of the Lord Jesus was greatly honored.* [18] *Many who became believers confessed their sinful practices.* [19] *A number of them who had been practicing sorcery brought their incantation books and burned them at a public bonfire. The value of the books was several million dollars.* [20] *So the message about the Lord spread widely and had a powerful effect.* — Acts 19:11-20

After Jesus ascended to heaven, He promised the Helper or the Holy Spirit would come to believers. It was the power of the Holy Spirit that enabled the disciples to continue to do miracles with the same power that Jesus displayed while on earth. Paul, the miracle worker in the previous verses, had actually been a religious leader who persecuted the newly established Christians. Until one day, Jesus met him and changed his life. Paul declared he believed Jesus was the Son of God who came to pay the price for his sins and was baptized in the Holy Spirit. The power Paul displayed, was the result of his faith in Jesus and his obedience to follow Him.

The next verses are about Peter, one of Jesus' disciples, and the power he displayed through the Holy Spirit.

> [12] *The apostles were performing many miraculous signs and wonders among the people. And all the believers were meeting regularly at the Temple in the area known as Solomon's Colonnade.* [13] *But no one else dared to join them, even though all the people had high regard for them.* [14] *Yet more and more people believed and were brought to the Lord—crowds of both men and women.* [15] *As a result of the apostles' work, sick people were brought out into the streets on beds and mats so that Peter's shadow might fall across some of them as he went by.* [16] *Crowds came from the villages around Jerusalem, bringing their sick and those possessed by evil spirits, and they were all healed.*
> — Acts 5:12-16

What does all this mean today? The power is available to everyone. The same miracle-working Holy Spirit who makes demons flee, is a free gift from the one true God to His children.

> [13] *And now you Gentiles have also heard the truth, the Good News that God saves you. And when you believed in Christ, he identified you as his own by giving you the Holy Spirit, whom he promised*

long ago. ¹⁴ The Spirit is God's guarantee that he will give us the inheritance he promised and that he has purchased us to be his own people. He did this so we would praise and glorify him. — Ephesians 1:13-14

Christians feel the power of the Holy Spirit who helps them through everything Satan attempts to inflict upon them. They know who their God is and where their help comes from. They understand that life on earth is very short compared to eternity and hold fast to the eternal life, free of evil, God has promised.

How do you stand up to Satan?

There are times Christians fall into patterns of endurance, because they let their power be diminished through compromise with the enemy as they allow something of Satan's to come into their lives. This creates constant lapses in the victories and joy that God promised. Restoration to God can only be experienced by drawing closer to Him.

There are those who find resisting and enduring isn't enough. Many Christians are fighters, and they don't like to give the enemy opportunities to torment them. There are verses in the book of Ephesians which advise to suit up for war each day. Not many take this seriously, but it's a serious, unequal war if fought without the power of God.

¹⁰ A final word: Be strong in the Lord and in his mighty power. ¹¹ Put on all of God's armor so that you will be able to stand firm against all strategies of the devil. [12] For we are not fighting against flesh-and-blood enemies, but against evil rulers and authorities of the unseen world, against mighty powers in this dark world, and against evil spirits in the heavenly places.

[13] Therefore, put on every piece of God's armor so you will be able to resist the enemy in the time of evil. Then after the battle you will still be standing firm. [14] Stand your ground, putting on the belt of truth and the body armor of God's righteousness. [15] For shoes, put on the peace that comes from the Good News so that you will be fully prepared. [16] In addition to all of these, hold up the shield of faith to stop the fiery arrows of the devil. [17] Put on salvation as your helmet, and take the sword of the Spirit, which is the word of God.
— Ephesians 6:10-17

Taking the steps to put on the armor of God may seem ridiculous to the physical eye; however, the Spiritual world takes note. God takes note. Satan takes note, and the demons take note because they know they can't penetrate the spiritual armor. It's as real to them as an impenetrable iron wall is to the human body.

Pray about all your concerns, but God wants a relationship. Talk to Him as if talking to a friend. Ask for answers. Ask for His advice. Satan will try to intervene at times you don't expect, so it's important to read the Bible and understand God's character. As understanding increases, the ability to recognize what is of God and what is of Satan also increases. This understanding is also called wisdom and discernment. Ask God for both.

Go to the throne of His grace with your petitions. First, ask for forgiveness of all sins, known and unknown. Ask God to forgive evil words, thoughts, and deeds. You can go before God because you are under the protective covering of the blood of His High Priest, Jesus. Ask the Lord to send His mighty warring angels against evil. THIS IS KEY: Remember evil is not the person, but Satan and the demons controlling the person. God loves all His children. God won't honor your request for an attack on someone. Judgment is eternal, and it's God's decision when He will judge a person. You can, however, call for war on the demons and ask God for protection from evil. When doing warfare, I ask for God's protection all the way out to my fringes. This protection begins with my inner circle, my family, and extends all the way out to the fringes, meaning the loved ones of my friends. If your requests are honorable, you will walk away having won your case in court against Satan's kingdom, and God will dispatch His angels to rectify the troubling situation. Elisha was a great prophet of God. He was in a battle against a physical kingdom driven by generations of powerful demons. God allowed Elisha's servant to see just how He had his back.

15 When the servant of the man of God got up early the next morning and went outside, there were troops, horses, and chariots everywhere. "Oh, sir, what will we do now?" the young man cried to Elisha.

¹⁶ "Don't be afraid!" Elisha told him. "For there are more on our side than on theirs!" ¹⁷ Then Elisha prayed, "O LORD, open his eyes and let him see!" The LORD opened the young man's eyes, and when he looked up, he saw that the hillside around Elisha was filled with horses and chariots of fire.

¹⁸ As the Aramean army advanced toward him, Elisha prayed, "O LORD, please make them blind." So the LORD struck them with blindness as Elisha had asked. — 2 Kings 6:15-18

Finally, as a last word, Psalm 91 is full of hope and promise of protection for those who choose God.

¹ Those who live in the shelter of the Most High will find rest in the shadow of the Almighty.

² This I declare about the LORD: He alone is my refuge, my place of safety; he is my God, and I trust him.

³ For he will rescue you from every trap and protect you from deadly disease.

⁴ He will cover you with his feathers. He will shelter you with his wings. His faithful promises are your armor and protection.

⁵ *Do not be afraid of the terrors of the night, nor the arrow that flies in the day.*

⁶ *Do not dread the disease that stalks in darkness, nor the disaster that strikes at midday.*

⁷ *Though a thousand fall at your side, though ten thousand are dying around you, these evils will not touch you.*

⁸ *Just open your eyes, and see how the wicked are punished.*

⁹ *If you make the LORD your refuge, if you make the Most High your shelter,*

¹⁰ *no evil will conquer you; no plague will come near your home.*

¹¹ *For he will order his angels to protect you wherever you go.*

¹² *They will hold you up with their hands so you won't even hurt your foot on a stone.*

¹³ *You will trample upon lions and cobras; you will crush fierce lions and serpents under your feet!*

¹⁴ *The LORD says, "I will rescue those who love me. I will protect those who trust in my name.*

¹⁵ *When they call on me, I will answer; I will be with them in trouble. I will rescue and honor them.*

¹⁶ *I will reward them with a long life and give them my salvation." — Psalm 91:1-16*

ENDNOTES

[1] https://en.wikipedia.org/wiki/Reptilians

[2] https://www.theatlantic.com/national/archive/2013/04/12-million-americans-believe-lizard-people-run-our-country/316706/

www.ingramcontent.com/pod-product-compliance
Lightning Source LLC
LaVergne TN
LVHW051231080426
835513LV00016B/1531